MIND
MAP
MASTERY

MIND MAP

TONY BUZAN

MASTERY

The **Complete Guide** to Learning and Using the
Most Powerful Thinking Tool in the Universe

WATKINS
Sharing Wisdom Since 1893

Mind Map Mastery
Tony Buzan

First published in the UK and USA in 2018 by
Watkins, an imprint of Watkins Media Limited
Unit 11, Shepperton House, 89 Shepperton Road
London N1 3DF

enquiries@watkinspublishing.com

Commissioning Editor: Chris Wold
Managing Editor: Fiona Robertson
Text Consultant and Editor: Sue Lascelles
Head of Design: Glen Wilkins
Designer: Clare Thorpe
Production: Uzma Taj
Commissioned Artwork: Joy Gosney

A CIP record for this book is available from the British Library

ISBN: 978-1-78678-141-3

10 9 8 7 6 5 4

Typeset in Helvetica Neue
Colour reproduction by XY Digital
Printed in China

www.watkinspublishing.com

Contents

Foreword

I have been using Mind Mapping for many years. Today, I travel the world, teaching business professionals, public figures and entire audiences to improve their memory and cognitive ability in their personal and professional lives. However, as a child I was diagnosed with dyslexia and I believe I had challenges – and still do to some degree – with attention. I have found that Mind Mapping is a great force to ward off the distraction of Attention Deficit Disorder. In short, it helps me stay on track.

Mind Maps are powerful tools for focusing and processing information, formulating a plan of action and getting started on new projects. In fact, Mind Mapping is a huge guiding hand in every aspect of life – and I can't recommend it highly enough!

As well as giving readers the means to transform their own lives, Tony's new book, *Mind Map Mastery*, will welcome them into a lively global community. The stories and examples show how Mind Mapping is a worldwide phenomenon that is practised by all types of people. The one thing they have in common is that they are passionate about the benefits of this thinking tool and go on to share it with others.

I remain immensely grateful to Tony for inventing the Mind Map, and would recommend his new book to anybody who wants to improve their thinking and achieve Mind Map mastery themselves.

Dominic O'Brien,
eight-time World Memory Champion and bestselling author

Preface

"I'm looking for books about using the brain."

"Try over there," the librarian said, gesturing toward a shelf of books, "in the medical section."

"No," I replied, "I've already gone through those titles and I've no desire to operate on my brain; I just want to learn how to use it."

The librarian looked at me blankly. "I'm afraid there aren't any books about that topic," she said. "Only the textbooks we have here."

I walked away feeling frustrated and astonished. In my second year at university, I was searching for new ways to cope with an increased academic workload, as my study methods simply weren't yielding the results I was after. In fact, the more notes I took, the worse I seemed to do. While I had yet to appreciate the true limits of linear thinking, that day I realized my so-called problem in fact represented an incredible opportunity. If there were no books about how to use the brain, then here was an area with extraordinary potential for research.

Over the years that followed, I studied psychology and the general sciences, neurophysiology, neurolinguistics and semantics, information theory, memory and mnemonic techniques, perception and creative thinking. I came to understand the workings of the human brain and the conditions that allow it to perform at its best.

Ironically, my research also highlighted the flaws in my own study methods, as it gradually dawned on me that my lecture notes were word-based, monotonic and boring; if anything, their linear format offered an incredibly effective way of training myself to be stupid! Practice makes perfect: if you practise perfectly, your practice makes you perfect. However, if you practise badly, practice makes you perfectly bad. When I began to practise more and more linear, monotonic note-taking, I became more and more perfectly stupid! I urgently needed to change both my thinking and my actions.

By studying the structure of the brain, I found the breakthrough I was searching for. The fact that we possess a minimum of 100 billion brain cells, each one of which contributes to our thinking, inspired me. I found it enthralling that each of these neurons has tentacles radiating out from the cell's centre like the branches of a tree, and I realized that I could make use of this model diagrammatically to create the ultimate thinking tool.

This proved to be a major contribution to the development of Radiant Thinking (see page 33), which in turn helped lead to the birth of the Mind Map.

At its simplest, a Mind Map is an intricate diagram that mirrors the structure of a brain cell with branches reaching out from its centre, evolving through patterns of association. However, since its inception in the mid-1960s, the Mind Map has proved to be much more than an excellent means of note-taking: it is an efficient and profoundly inspiring way to feed our starving minds, intellects and spirits. It has developed exponentially and, as you will see in this book, can be applied in many ways – from nurturing creativity and strengthening memory to helping fight dementia.

Over the years, the Mind Map has been misunderstood by some and misrepresented by others, yet my vision persists of a world in which every child and adult understands what a Mind Map is, how it works, and how it can be applied to all aspects of life.

This book aims to show you how a good Mind Map can feed you as an individual, and how the Mind Map itself continues to grow, expand and evolve in order to tackle the new challenges we all face on this planet.

And now, as we advance into the 21st century, the Mind Map can be accessed and utilized in new forms that mirror our burgeoning new technical possibilities. Mind Maps can still be hand drawn, of course, but they can also be generated by computer program, they are available online, they have been traced in the Arctic snow, they have adorned the sides of mountains and they can even be etched by drones in the sky.

Join me in this great adventure and prepare to radiate your mental power far beyond anything you have ever experienced before!

TONY BUZAN

Introduction

Why Is This Book Needed?

A Mind Map is a revolutionary thinking tool that, when mastered, will transform your life. It will help you process information, come up with new ideas, strengthen your memory, get the most out of your leisure time and improve the way you work.

I devised the Mind Map initially as an innovative form of note-taking that can be used in any situation where linear notes would normally be taken, such as attending lectures, listening to telephone calls, during business meetings, carrying out research and studying. However, it quickly became clear that Mind Maps can also be used for ground-breaking design and planning; for providing an incisive overview of a subject; for inspiring new projects; for uncovering solutions and breaking free from unproductive ways of thinking, among many other things. In this book, you will come across innumerable exciting applications for Mind Maps. They can even be used as an exercise in their own right to give your brain a workout and boost your powers of creative thinking.

In *Mind Map Mastery*, you will discover how Mind Mapping can help you access your own multiple intelligences and realize your true potential. The practical exercises in this book are designed to train you in this expansive way of thinking, and you will discover the true stories of other people, including master Mind Mappers and world-renowned experts and pioneers in their fields, whose lives have been radically transformed by Mind Mapping.

Your brain is a sleeping giant, and *Mind Map Mastery* is here to help wake it up!

A New Way of Thinking

When I introduced Mind Maps to the world in the 1960s, little did I suspect what lay ahead. In the preliminary stages of my research into human thinking, I used an early prototype of Mind Mapping to improve my studies. This was a form of note-taking in which I combined words and colours. It evolved when I started to underline the keywords in my notes and realized they made up less than 10 percent of what I had written down. Yet these keywords unlocked core concepts. Through my study of the ancient Greeks, I knew I needed to find a simple way to make connections between the keywords so that they could be easily memorized.

The ancient Greeks developed a number of elaborate memory systems that enabled them to perfectly recall hundreds and thousands of facts. These systems relied on the power of imagination and association to make connections through, for example, the method of loci. This was one of the techniques invented by the ancient Greeks to improve their memories and is also known as the Memory Journey, the Memory Palace or the Mind Palace Technique (see box, *right*).

I came across the method of loci during my research into human thought processes, but I had been unwittingly introduced to another mnemonic method in the very first minutes of my very first day at university. This was the Major System – a phonetic method developed by the German writer and historian Johann Just Winckelmann (1620–99). In the first lecture of my university term, a sardonic professor, built like a barrel with tufts of red hair sprouting from his head, walked into the lecture room and, hands clasped behind his back, proceeded to call out the roll of students perfectly. If somebody was absent, he called out their name, the names of their parents, and the student's date of birth, phone number and home address. When he had finished, he looked at us with a raised eyebrow and a slight sneer. He despised his students, but he was a marvellous teacher – and I was hooked.

How to Build a Memory Palace

According to the Roman orator Cicero (106–43 BCE), the spatial memorization technique known as the method of loci (or places, from the Latin *loci*) was discovered by a Greek lyric poet and *sophos* (wise man) called Simonides of Ceos (*c*.556–*c*.468 BCE).

In his dialogue *De Oratore*, Cicero describes how Simonides attended a banquet to perform a poem in honour of the host. Shortly after performing the poem, he was called outside and while he was gone the roof of the banqueting hall suddenly collapsed, crushing the other guests to death. Some of their bodies were mangled beyond recognition, which was a great concern, as they needed to be identified in order to receive the proper burial rites. Simonides, however, was able to identify the dead by drawing on his visual memory of where each of the guests had been seated around the banquet table.

From this experience, Simonides realized that anyone could improve their memory by selecting locations and forming mental images of the things they wished to remember. If the images were stored in the visualized places in a particular order, it would then be possible to remember anything through the power of association. The resulting method of loci was described in a number of the rhetorical treatises of ancient Greece and Rome, and is better known to us today as the Memory Palace.

When, after that first lecture, I asked him how he'd managed to perform such an extraordinary feat of memory, he refused to tell me, simply saying, "Son, I'm a genius." I tested him for the next three months until one day he decided to let us in on his secret, and taught us the Major System. This mnemonic technique uses a simple code that converts numbers into phonetic sounds. The sounds can then be turned into words – and the words transformed into images with which to furnish a Memory Palace.

My new method of note-taking drew upon my growing understanding of mnemonic systems and radically simplified the practice of the ancient Greeks by using colour to forge links between interrelated concepts. While it had yet to evolve into a fully fledged Mind Map, it was already markedly more effective than straightforward linear note-taking, which by comparison was monochromatic, monotone and monotonous – with the results to match. If you are making notes using only blue or black ink, the effect of the print on the page is by default boring, which means your brain will tune out, dial down and eventually go to sleep. All of which explains why "sleeping sickness" often plagues study halls, libraries and meetings!

Pleased with the success of my new method, I began to take on pupils as a hobby and coach them in my technique. Many of my pupils had been labelled as academic failures and it was rewarding to watch them quickly start to improve their grades and outperform their peers (see box, *right*).

The Next Steps

During the subsequent stages of my development of Mind Maps, I began to think in more detail about the hierarchy that governs our patterns of thinking, and I realized that there are

key ideas ➡ key **key** ideas ➡ key **key key** ideas

Buzzing about "Buzan Diagrams"

Jezz Moore was a struggling college student when he attended a lecture on a new method of learning called "Buzan Diagrams". The lecturer explained how to write down a topic in the centre of the page and fill the area around it with "keywords" and "prompts" that were strung together with connecting lines, thereby dispensing with the need to memorize elaborate lists. Jezz was stunned by how simple yet effective this method was. From being an academic underachiever, he went on to read economics and politics at university and, after post-graduate studies in corporate finance, gained a Master of Business Administration (MBA).

Some years later, he found himself at a rowing club supper. The subject of learning and education came up, and Jezz – fuelled by his passion for the technique that had transformed his studies, as well as a glass or two of wine – began to lecture the guest sitting next to him on how "being clever is easy". Inviting his fellow guest to interrupt if he was going too fast, he explained how the technique worked and helpfully sketched a diagram on a paper napkin: "There you have it … Buzan Diagrams." A moment lapsed before the guest said, "You do realize I am Tony Buzan?"

I was delighted to hear first-hand how my note-taking methods had helped change Jezz's life; and Jezz and I have since become the best of friends. In the years that followed, I used Mind Mapping techniques to help Jezz coach athletes who went on to row for Great Britain and to become Olympic medallists.

In this way, I discovered the power of Radiant Thinking, which I will explain in more detail in Chapter 1 (see page 33). As my understanding grew, I gradually began to build up the architecture of the Mind Map using connections such as arrows, codes and curving lines. A pivotal meeting with the talented Australian landscape artist Lorraine Gill helped me formulate the next steps, as she challenged me to reappraise the role that pictures and colours played within the Mind Map's structure. Her insights inspired the ways in which imagery is used in Mind Maps today.

When I compared my evolving techniques with notes made by historical figures such as the Renaissance artists Leonardo da Vinci (1452–1519) and Michelangelo (1475–1564), and scientists such as Madame Curie (1867–1934) and Einstein (1879–1955), I found some interesting parallels in the ways in which they used pictures, codes and interconnecting lines: their words and diagrams explode in all directions across the page, free to roam in whichever direction their thoughts happen to take, rather than remaining glued to a straight horizontal line. (See also "A Short History of the Thinking Behind Mind Maps", page 42.) However, the real-life experiences of my growing number of students, clients and colleagues suggested that the techniques I was developing were so accessible, they could help people from all walks of life: you didn't have to be a world-class genius making ground-breaking discoveries to benefit from them.

Mind Maps are analytical in the sense that you can use them to solve any problem. Through the use of associated logic, Mind Maps delve right to the heart of the matter. They also allow you to see the bigger picture. They are on the one hand microcosmic and on the other macrocosmic.

Keeping It Natural

I described in the Preface how, during the course of my research, I was struck by the shape of a brain cell itself: notes jotted down in diagram form often seemed, albeit unwittingly, to mimic the organic structure of a neuron, with connecting branches reaching from a nucleus.

While I was mulling this over, I would go for long walks in nature, where my thoughts and imagination felt much freer to wander. It dawned on me that as we humans are part of nature, our thinking and note-taking ought to reflect nature too in some way: we should reflect the laws of nature in all our human functioning, especially when it comes to putting outside the brain what is found within it.

I gradually developed my techniques into a thinking tool that could be applied to a whole range of human daily activities, and that would mirror the creativity and radiance of our thought processes. The result was the first true Mind Map.

Conventional Note-taking vs Mind Mapping

The box below shows the key characteristics of linear note-taking set against those of Mind Mapping.

Conventional Note-taking	Mind Mapping
Linear	Multi-faceted
Monochrome	Colourful
Word-based	Words combined with pictures
Listed logic	Associated logic
Sequential	Multidimensional
Restrictive	Imaginative
Disorganized	Analytical

Going Forward

Today, people all around the globe are familiar with the concept of Mind Mapping. In addition to Mind Mapping conferences, World Mind Mapping Championships have been held in the UK, Singapore, China and many other countries. During the Championships, various disciplines are tested. Competitors are, for example, invited to create Mind Maps while listening to a lecture on an unfamiliar subject, or on a set text. The results are then marked according to 20 different criteria, such as the impact of the imagery, the use of humour (for instance, through puns), the attractiveness of the Mind Map and its originality, and whether it obeys the fundamental principles of Mind Mapping.

With the spread of the Mind Map and the resulting improved global mental literacy, it could be assumed that the case for Mind Mapping is all wrapped up by now – that the Mind Map is protected and secure, and there is little more to be said about it. Yet sadly that is not the case.

While it is true that there have been some wonderful realizations of my original dream that every man, woman and child should discover the benefits of Mind Mapping, there have also been some problems. Over recent decades, the Mind Map has at times been misunderstood and misappropriated by those who purport to be trained teachers in the art of Mind Mapping, but whose understanding of the process turns out to be fundamentally flawed, and whose practice therefore doesn't follow the key Laws of Mind Mapping that you will find in Chapter 2 (see page 60). Whenever Mind Mapping is mistaught, I believe there is a risk that ultimately the purity and power of the Mind Map itself will be compromised.

Fortunately, however, the Mind Map is a robust entity. It is, after all, an evolutionary form of thinking, perfectly adapted to the requirements of our digital age – and beyond.

How to Use This Book

Mind Map Mastery will show you how to use this powerful tool in your own life wherever it takes you. This book is structured so that you can read it from cover to cover and also keep dipping into it as an ongoing source of reference:

Chapter 1: What Is a Mind Map? will introduce you to the key principles underlying the Mind Map, setting out its essential ingredients and explaining why Mind Mapping works. This chapter also sketches a brief history of the Mind Map from early civilization to today.

Chapter 2: How to Mind Map offers practical exercises, useful tips and training in how to use Mind Mapping effectively. It sets out the Laws of Mind Mapping and looks at practical applications for Mind Maps in everyday life, including at home, work, in education and for creativity, wellbeing and memory.

Chapter 3: What Is *Not* a Mind Map? clears up some common misconceptions about what the Mind Map is and what it isn't, and aims to tackle any confusion surrounding this incredible tool.

Chapter 4: Solution Finding considers which steps to take if you are trying to create Mind Maps but still can't seem to make them work for you. It tackles related issues such as Mind Mapping and indecision, and offers Mind Mapping workouts.

Chapter 5: The Infinite Applications of Mind Maps
explains the incredible scope of Mind Maps and how they
can be used at a more advanced level. It offers further
guidance and inspiring insights into how to use Mind Maps
in innovative ways to transform your own life.

Chapter 6: The Future of Mind Mapping considers
Mind Mapping in a digital age and its relationship with
Artificial Intelligence, while looking toward the future.

I cannot imagine my life without Mind Maps. I use them every day, whether
I'm lecturing, planning my week or writing articles and books! They have
changed my world in more ways than I could ever have conceived possible.
I believe that *Mind Map Mastery* can do the same for you too.

For those of you who are completely new to this technique, you are about to
discover an amazing tool with the potential to blow your mind! For those of
you who are already familiar with Mind Mapping, while this book makes no
claims to reinvent the wheel of Mind Maps, it will surely put some powerful
new tyres on it and take you places you'd never imagined.

**It's now time to set out on your own Mind Mapping adventure and
discover the incredible power of your brain …**

1

What Is a Mind Map?

This chapter introduces the wonderful world of Mind Maps. It explains exactly what a Mind Map is and the key ingredients in this incredible thinking tool, as well as the essential steps to creating one. You will discover the Mind Map's place in history, and how Mind Maps relate to the workings of the human brain. Most importantly, you will begin to understand how Mind Maps allow you to unlock your true potential.

Whole-brain Thinking

Both the beauty and the impact of this holistic thinking tool lie in its simplicity. On paper, it is a colourful visual diagram used to capture information. However, it does this in a way that appeals to the cortical workings of the brain. It activates "whole-brain" thinking, engaging both the logical left-hand side of the brain and its creative right-hand hemisphere.

The notion of the brain's two divided ways of thinking was first popularized by American artist Betty Edwards in her ground-breaking book *Drawing on the Right Side of the Brain*. Published in 1979, the book was based on Dr Edwards' understanding of neuroscience, in particular the Nobel Prize-winning work of Dr Roger W. Sperry (1913–94), which she used to introduce a revolutionary way of drawing and teaching. She argued that the brain has two ways of perceiving and processing reality: the left side of the brain is verbal and analytical, while the right side is visual and perceptual. Her teaching method was designed to bypass the censorship of the brain's analytical left-hand side and to free up the expressiveness of the right hemisphere. She went on to found the Center for the Educational Applications of Brain Hemisphere Research, and her work continues to influence artists and teachers around the world today.

Left brain
Logic
Numbers
Sequence
Analysis
Words
Lists

Right brain
Spatial awareness
Imagination
Colour
Holistic awareness
Daydreaming
Dimension

Functions controlled by the left brain and the right brain

How to Create a Mind Map

So what does Mind Mapping look like in practice? Let's start by making a basic Mind Map.

GETTING STARTED
You will need:

- ✔ **A large sheet of plain white paper**
- ✔ **A selection of coloured pens or pencils**
- ✔ **A brain**
- ✔ **An open mind**
- ✔ **Imagination**
- ✔ **A subject that you wish to explore**

A good Mind Map has three essential characteristics:

1. A central image that captures the main subject under consideration. For example, if you were using a Mind Map to plan a project, you could put a sketch of a folder in the centre. No special artistic skill is needed to create a good Mind Map.

2. Thick branches radiating out from the central image. These branches represent the key themes relating to the main subject, and each one is represented by a different colour. In turn, the main branches sprout subsidiary branches – twigs, if you like, in the form of second- and third-level branches – which relate to further associated themes.

3. A single key image or word is placed on each branch.

Step 1

Place the sheet of paper in front of you in landscape format (i.e. horizontally). Next, use at least three different colours to draw an image in the very centre of the paper that represents the subject you would like to consider, which in this example is the plays of William Shakespeare (1564–1616). If you don't want to draw the Bard's head, you could sketch a quill pen or some other simple symbol instead. The central image will activate your imagination and trigger associations in your thoughts. If you want a word at the centre, make it appear multidimensional and combine it with an image.

Step 2

Now pick a colour and draw a thick branch coming away from the central image, like the bough of a tree. You can do this by sketching two lines that radiate out from the centre and then connect them at the tip. Let the branch curve organically, as this will be visually engaging and therefore more interesting to the brain, making you more likely to memorize the information on the branch. Shade in the branch. Its thickness symbolizes the weight of this association in the hierarchy of your Mind Map.

Step 3

Label the branch with a single word in capital letters. As this Mind Map is about Shakespeare's plays, you might label this first branch "COMEDY", or "TRAGEDY" or "HISTORY". Alternatively, instead of writing a word, you might decide to draw a comedic mask, a dagger or a crown.

1

2

3

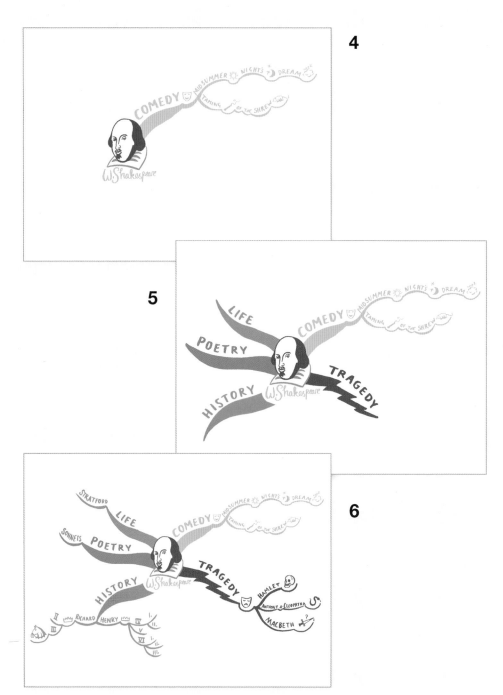

Step 4

Send out secondary-level shoots
from the main branch. Then draw third-
level branches that spread out from these
secondary-level shoots. Write keywords
on all the branches or draw symbols, or a
combination of both. Give each symbol its
own branch. There's no need to rush: leave
some of the branches empty at first, as this
will naturally inspire your brain to fill them in.

Step 5

Pick another colour and create your next
main branch, working around the central
image. (Many beginners find it easiest to
work clockwise around the centre, but do
whatever suits you best.) As before, draw
secondary- and third-level branches from
this new branch and label them. Keep
adding main branches until you have
about five or six of them to work with.

Step 6

Now you have your main branches,
move freely around your Mind Map, leaping
from branch to branch, filling in any gaps
and adding new sub-branches as ideas
and associations occur to you.

7

Step 7

If you wish, add arrows, curving lines and links between your main branches to reinforce the connections between them.

Et voilà! – you have created your first Mind Map.

Taking It Further

The example that I've included here is still a work in progress at this stage and could be expanded to include all of Shakespeare's 37 plays, his sonnets and narrative poems, as well as key facts relating to his life and times. If you are interested in the playwright – or if you like a challenge – you could have a go at completing your own version of this Mind Map. Then, once you have memorized the information in it, you will have facts about one of the world's most famous writers available at your fingertips and be able to impress people with your knowledge of the Bard!

As Mind Mapping involves the workings of both sides of the brain, it is multifunctional and can be applied to all cognitive functions, including memory, creativity, learning and all forms of thinking. This is one reason why it has been described as "the Swiss army knife for the brain". It is useful, practical – and fun!

The Essential Ingredients

We have seen how a Mind Map can take a single central concept and unpack it creatively and efficiently, allowing us to discover new associations and forge connections between ideas in memorable ways. Yet what precisely are the key ingredients that make Mind Mapping such a powerful thinking tool?

While we have already touched upon some of these elements, it's well worth exploring the key ingredients – Radiant Thinking, non-linear organic flow, colour, images and words – in a little more detail.

RADIANT THINKING

Radiant Thinking plays an integral part in the formation of Mind Maps, but before we explore it, I would like to ask you a quick question:

What is your prime language?

Just hold that thought. And be prepared to realize that you've got the answer wrong.

Now, let me introduce you to a wonderful mental game, which has already changed the lives of thousands of people around the world …

When I asked you about your prime language, think about your answer. In all likelihood, the answer you gave was wrong. Your prime language isn't English, Dutch, Cantonese or one of the other 7,096 living languages listed in the Ethnologue catalogue.

> **Your prime language is the Human Language itself, which is shared by all humankind and is the natural language of babies in the womb!**

We are in fact all fluent in the Human Language from birth. From birth to the age of about four months old, a baby begins to focus on objects that are about 20–25cm (8–10in) away – the distance to the parent's face. For most babies, the first central image they have of the world is the face of their mother, and radiating out from the central image of the mother's face are umpteen associations to do with food, love, warmth, health, sleep and survival. In this way, we are hardwired from birth to perceive the world through Mind Mapping.

Human Language is the language spoken by the workings of the brain and is primarily formed by the combined powers of "imagination" and "association", with a sub-branch of "location". (The importance of location explains why the position of the branches on your Mind Map helps you to memorize them.)

Self-Examination Exercise

In a moment I will give you a word, and ask you to close your eyes and allow your brain's super biocomputer to engage. Then, when you've read the word, check how long it takes you to understand it, what information your brain gives you about it, and whether there are any colours or associations connected with it. Here goes …

The word for you is:
PINEAPPLE

Did your supercomputer give you a nice printout with the letters
P-I-N-E-A-P-P-L-E
neatly spelled out? I'm guessing not …

Quickly jot down your responses to the following:
- **What did your supercomputer give you?**
- **How long did it take your computer to access this data?**
- **What associations did it give you?**
- **What else came to mind?**
- **Which colours were linked with it?**
- **Did it make you think of anything else, such as texture, taste, scent or location?**

My prediction is that you will have received a picture, or even a set of images with multisensory associations and colours.

If that's the case, welcome to the human race!

Like the mass of florets in a dandelion head, your thinking radiates outward, creating associations from associations.

All spoken and written languages are beautiful, important and vital. They are, however, secondary languages or subroutines. The Human Language, formed of imagination and association, is *the* primary language of our species. Look at the illustration *opposite*. This represents how your brain and every other human's brain thinks. Pretty mind-blowing, isn't it?

By reacting to the word "pineapple" through a multitude of spontaneous associations, you have just demonstrated the ways in which your brain offers an infinite number of opportunities for thought, memory and creativity. Your thinking is Radiant! It has an infinite number of radials, and each radial has the ability to subdivide into another infinite number of radials – the process continuing ad infinitum.

Socrates, the Gadfly of Athens

The classical Greek philosopher Socrates (*c.*470–399BC) famously said, "The unexamined life is not worth living." While some people thought Socrates looked more like a satyr than a man, few disputed the splendour of his mind. He challenged the citizens of Athens to think deeply, and like a gadfly "stung" the state into performing its duties. He showed the value of unpacking an idea, layer by layer. This principle of sticking with an argument through all its ramifications also underlies the Mind Map, which can be used to explore an idea to the full through its branches.

Human Language can be externalized. And when it is externalized in its purest form, it creates a Mind Map.

By allowing ideas to radiate out from the core concept, a Mind Map encourages a highly personalized response to a concept. Its radiant structure makes it easier to spot connections between different branches of the map and to generate fresh associations in order to fill in any blank spaces, thereby encouraging us to carry on thinking creatively for longer.

NON-LINEAR ORGANIC FLOW

I described earlier how I realized as a student that linear note-taking was effectively a means of training myself to be stupid. Linear thinking, such as adding new items to a list in a linear sequence, actually limits your thinking. As you get further down a list, for example, your creativity begins to dwindle and you stop thinking imaginatively or inventively. Consequently, linearity will very likely undermine your ability to access or retain all the information that is available to you.

The human brain does not think in toolbars, menus and lists; it thinks organically.

Imagine the veins in a leaf, the branches of a tree or even the complex network of the human nervous system: this is how the brain thinks. Therefore, to think well, the brain needs a tool that reflects a natural organic flow – which is where the structure of the Mind Map comes into its own. The Mind Map marks the next step in the progression from linear ("one-dimensional") thinking, through to lateral ("two-dimensional") thought, to multi-dimensional thinking or Radiant Thought.

Mind Maps mimic the myriad synapses and connections of our own brain cells, thereby reflecting the way we ourselves are created and connected (see also "Internal Mind Maps", page 53). Like us, the natural world is forever changing and regenerating, and has a communication structure that mirrors our own. A Mind Map is thus a thinking tool that draws upon the inspiration and effectiveness of these natural structures. Its organic properties are embodied in the curvilinear nature of its branches, which, as we have seen, are more appealing to the brain than straight lines.

COLOUR

When, as a student, I introduced two different colours into my note-taking, I improved my memory of those notes by more than 100 percent. Why was this?

Colour relates to the right-hand side of the brain, whereas words are associated with the rational left-hand hemisphere. So a combination of colour and words engages the workings of both sides of the brain.

In addition to this, the introduction of colour made me begin to enjoy the note-taking process – and fun is a vital part of Mind Mapping. Colours stimulate memory and creativity, freeing us from the trap of monochrome monotony. They add life to images and make them more attractive. They can inspire us to explore and make an impact on how we communicate with others. Numerous studies show how a considered use of colour can:

- **Capture attention**
- **Greatly improve comprehension**
- **Ignite motivation**
- **Encourage vibrant communication**
- **Increase the mental processing and storing of images**

Colour can also act as a code. If you use specific colours to depict different areas and themes within a Mind Map, you will create a visual shorthand that will enable you to memorize the information in that Mind Map much more easily, and significantly improve your recall.

In 1933, the German psychiatrist and paediatrician Hedwig von Restorff (1906–62) conducted a study in which she found that participants were better at remembering items that stood out from their surroundings in some way. Imagine, for example, a list of boys' names that includes the girl's name "Heidi" highlighted in orange. The chances are that you will remember "Heidi", as it stands out from the context as being a girl's name in a different colour.

In Mind Maps, colour and symbols can similarly be used to activate the von Restorff effect, or "isolation effect" as it is also known, by making different branches stand out from their surroundings in some way.

Make life colourful with Mind Maps!

IMAGES

When we are young, we usually learn to draw before we can write. The history of human mark-making has parallels with this process, with the first manmade marks appearing in the form of cave art and evolving over millennia – via pictograms and hieroglyphs – into the written word. (See the following pages for "A Short History of the Thinking Behind Mind Maps".)

Unlike words, images have an immediacy about them: visual information is processed by the brain 60,000 times faster than text. In addition to this, images stimulate the imagination, are rich in associations and transcend the limits of verbal communication. (Just think of the effectiveness of all the road signs around the world.) Like colour, they encourage harmony between the left- and right-hand sides of the brain, balancing our linguistic skills with visual skills. They also make use of other cortical skills, such as form, line and dimensionality.

The saying "a picture is worth a thousand words" has been scientifically proven by the likes of American psychologists Professor Ralph Haber and Professor Raymond S. Nickerson. Images really are more effective than words in engaging our brains. To give the images in your Mind Maps even more impact, keep them crisp, colourful and clear. This will make them attractive, engaging and memorable.

WORDS

A genuine Mind Map uses single words on its branches. This is because single words pack more of a punch than a phrase, as each individual word will trigger its own unique set of associations and thereby generate new ideas. By comparison, a phrase is a fixed entity, stuck in its compound meaning rather than open to free association, and its impact is therefore diluted.

If you feel you absolutely have to use a phrase, break it down so that each word within that phrase is strung separately on the branch and given the freedom to sprout its own sub-branches. Better still, keep to single words.

One word per branch of your Mind Map will make your brain really engage with the subject and go to the heart of the matter. It will give your brain a hook on which to hang a memory.

A Short History of the Thinking Behind Mind Maps

Like anything that strikes us as being completely new, different or innovative, the Mind Map did not appear completely out of the blue, or land on this planet like some sort of alien spacecraft. As will be clear by now, I didn't wake up one morning and invent Mind Mapping on a whim. The Mind Map is a natural evolution of human thinking.

Mind Maps arise naturally from the process through which human beings have attempted since ancient times to use imagery to share their innermost thoughts. In fact, the roots of the Mind Map can be traced back to the earliest marks deliberately made by the very first artists on cave walls some 40,000 years ago. Both art and writing are expressions of thought made visible, and attitudes toward these practices, as well as the balance between them, have influenced the expression of ideas throughout history – from the Stone Age to the 21st century.

CAVE ART

The invention of symbolic expression was one of the great innovations in the history of humankind. An early form of art appeared in the shape of

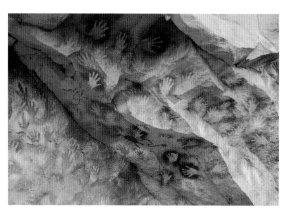

Hand stencils, possibly 9,000 years old, in the Cueva de las Manos, Santa Cruz, Argentina.

hand stencils. There is a theory that, by using pigments to trace the outlines of hands on cave walls, our ancestors discovered how a three-dimensional object could be represented by a two-dimensional line. They then depicted the outlines of animals such as horses, bison and deer in cave paintings.

SUMERIAN CUNEIFORM

In c.3,500 BCE, the Sumerians developed a primitive form of accountancy in order to keep tallies of their agricultural produce and livestock, keeping their accounts on clay tablets. They went on to abstract the outlines of animals into small lines and shapes, which were similarly transcribed. These pictograms formed the basis of the earliest known writing script.

Administrative record in Sumerian cuneiform, the world's oldest script.

EGYPTIAN HIEROGLYPHS

The hieroglyphs developed in the Second Dynasty of ancient Egypt (c.2890–2670 BCE) were based on pictures. While some represented the objects they depicted, it was more usual for hieroglyphs to be used as phonograms. This means their sounds convey meaning, rather than their shapes. This led to a divide between a word as it appears visually and the objects it refers to, allowing for the study of abstract concepts and lending fresh weight to the power of association in the development of ideas.

Hieroglyphics in the tomb of Thutmose III in the Valley of the Kings, Luxor, Egypt.

Roman copy of the Aphrodite of Knidos by ancient Greek sculptor Praxiteles.

ANCIENT GREECE

Over the course of several centuries, the ancient Greeks refined the visual language of thought, as is evident in the evolution of their art from the static, formalized kouros statues of the Archaic period to the much more realistic human figures created by sculptors such as Praxiteles in the 4th century BCE. A groundbreaking artist, Praxiteles is believed to have been the first to represent the naked female form as a freestanding lifesize statue.

The ancient Greeks' three-dimensional approach to the world and questioning of our place in it was reflected in the work of many thinkers, including Euclid (*c.*300 BCE), Archimedes (*c.*287–212 BCE), Eratosthenes (*c.*275–194 BCE), Socrates (*c.*469–399 BCE), Plato (*c.*429–347 BCE), Aristotle (*c.*384–322 BCE) and Phidias (5th century BCE). These innovators were not content to accept the world at face value, but instead pushed the boundaries of thinking in much the way that modern Mind Map allows us to do today.

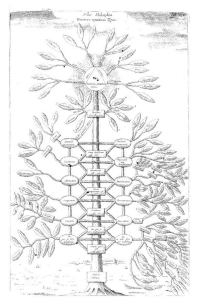

Arbor Porphyriana **by the 6th-century philosopher Boethius.**

TREELIKE DIAGRAMS

Although the fall of the Roman Empire took place in the 5th century CE, Latin continued to exert an influence over Western thought. Its adoption and adaptation by the Christian Church reinforced a cultural belief in the superiority of the written word as the primary channel for thought, creativity and communication. However, philosophers such as Boethius (*c*.480–524/525 CE) used treelike diagrams such as the *Arbor Porphyriana* as teaching devices to explore categories; and elaborate medieval drawings of the "Tree of Jesse", listing the ancestors of Christ, were also used as mnemonic aids, combining words and images.

LEONARDO DA VINCI

Renaissance artist and inventor Leonardo da Vinci (1452–1519) has an important place in the history of the development of Mind Mapping. Leonardo's notes juxtapose sketches, symbols and words, combining imagination, association and analysis, and revealing how his incredible creativity was supported by the full range of his brain's skills.

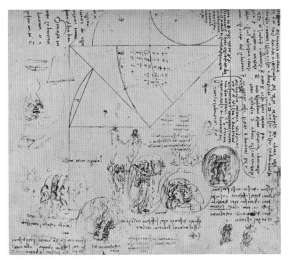

Page from da Vinci's notebook (*c*.1480), mixing words, geometry, images and symbols.

45

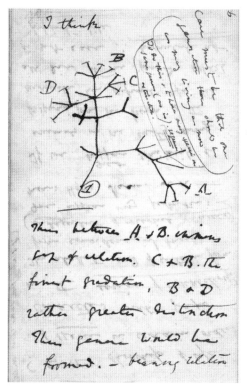

Darwin's sketch (c.1837) exploring his idea of an evolutionary tree for the first time.

CHARLES DARWIN (1809–82)

The British naturalist Charles Darwin created what may be one of the most important proto-Mind Maps ever drawn. In his "Tree of Life" sketch, he maps out his first thoughts on how species might be related through evolutionary history. Modern geneticists have found that, in fact, species crossbreed more than Darwin originally thought. This interconnected thinking is reflected in today's Mind Maps, which create links between different branches with arrows and lines.

ALBERT EINSTEIN (1879–1955)

In a newspaper interview in 1929, German-born American theoretical physicist Albert Einstein stated: "I am enough of the artist to draw freely upon my imagination. Imagination is more important than knowledge. Knowledge is limited. Imagination encircles the world." Einstein's thinking was diagrammatic and schematic, rather than linear and verbal, making him the 20th-century godfather of Mind Mapping.

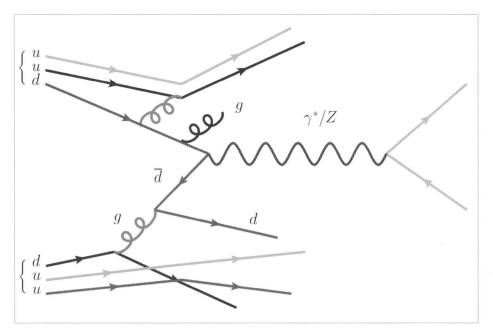

Feynman diagram depicting the behaviour of subatomic particles.

RICHARD FEYNMAN (1918–88)

The American Nobel Prize-winning physicist Richard Feynman introduced the first Feynman diagram to the world in 1949. As a young man, Feynman understood the importance of visualization and imagination to the creative thinking process, and taught himself to draw. He went on to devise pictorial representations of the mathematical formula used to describe the behaviour of subatomic particles, which became known as Feynman diagrams. He was so taken with these diagrams that he covered his van in them!

Mind Mapping in Practice

After all these centuries, our attitude to images and words continues to evolve. Today, there are some signs of a shift away from dominant verbal forms of communication toward visual thinking (as evidenced by the growing popularity of emojis as a form of visual shorthand), which is perhaps redressing an imbalance that existed in previous decades. In academic forums, for example, words have traditionally been accorded precedence over images – with, as we have seen, some notable exceptions appearing in the work of giants such as Feynman and Einstein. Once again, however, the power of the image is coming to the fore in all our communications: we increasingly use our phones as cameras – to capture scenes rather than share dialogue, and document the minutiae of our lives in pictures on social media; we think, work and interact with complete strangers around the world, and are therefore becoming more reliant on technologies that allow us to transcend spoken-language barriers.

By marrying words and images, and by mirroring the workings of the human brain in its combination of logical and creative input, the Mind Map is the perfect tool for our globalized 21st century.

Some Mind Maps are very simple and direct, while others are incredibly elaborate. *Opposite* is an example that is a simple but true Mind Map, created according to the Laws of Mind Mapping (see Chapter 2, page 60). It's a simple Mind Map for planning a vacation. Note how each word or image sits on its own branch, how each branch has its own colour, and how playful imagery, which captures the excitement of planning a summer trip, makes this Mind Map fun to create and easy to remember. The main branches relate to the key considerations of planning a vacation: where to

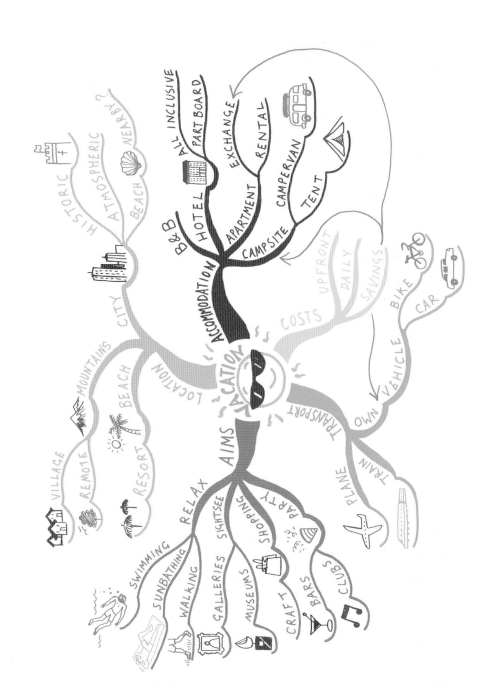

go, where to stay, the cost, how to get there and what the main aims of the trip are. The Mind Map's sub-branches delve more deeply into all these aspects – for example, considering mountains versus city versus beach resorts as possible destinations, and detailing the different accommodation and transport options available. One sub-branch of costs looks at savings and this is linked by arrows to some cheaper options.

If you are unsure about the sort of vacation you want, creating a Mind Map like this will help you think through all the alternatives, weigh up issues such as cost versus aims, and come to a conclusion about what you really want to do.

A Mind Map will:

- **Offer you clarity and an overview of a subject**
- **Give you the information you need to help you plan ahead**
- **Provide a full review of a situation**
- **Act as a massive storehouse for information**
- **Activate your imagination, encouraging you to find creative solutions**
- **Be a pleasure to look at in its own right**

The Many Advantages of Mind Mapping

As well as offering a clear overview of a subject and providing a visual tool to will help you to memorize it, Mind Mapping has many other advantages:

Thinking: Use Mind Mapping to ignite your brain, come up with fresh ideas and associations, and create a colourful record of your thinking processes.

Learning: Mind Maps make great study aids, useful for note-taking during classes and lectures, as well as for exam revision. A Mind Map cuts through the dead wood to highlight the key branches of any topic.

Concentrating: Mind Mapping means focusing closely on the task in hand, engaging your brain in a way that will inevitably lead to better results.

Organizing: Use Mind Maps for parties, weddings, trips, family gatherings and even your future life.

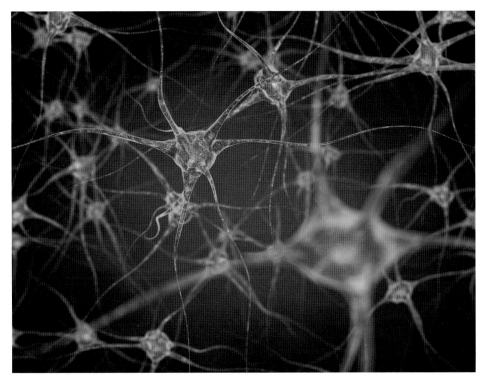

A Mind Map's structure mimics the brain's network of synapses and neural paths.

Planning: Prioritize your time and commitments by using Mind Mapping to plan your diary and schedule.

Communicating: Cut through the waffle and communicate with precision – a Mind Map will highlight the essential points that you need to get across.

Speaking: Dispense with pages of notes by making information available at a glance, keeping your presentations and speeches clear, relaxed and dynamic.

Leading: Create excellent business tools, whether setting an agenda, taking the minutes or chairing a meeting. The Mind Map gives you a control desk for making sense of your internal and external universes.

Training: Chuck out the wordy manuals and use Mind Maps to plan training programmes in a quick and accessible format.

Negotiating: See all your options, available strategies and potential outcomes laid out clearly on one page. The Mind Map will help you to negotiate a win–win result.

Mind Maps and the Brain

We have seen how Mind Maps work organically like the brain, mimicking the ways in which new pathways are formed or consolidated when information is passed between branches and brain cells. By stimulating Radiant Thinking, a Mind Map exaggerates the brain's natural functions, making the brain stronger, more creative and more effective. The human brain contains more than a billion neurons, or nerve cells, each one of which is more powerful than a home computer. Yet through the power of Radiant Thinking, the brain operates synergetically rather than linearly. This means the sum of its operations is always greater than its parts.

Moreover, Mind Maps mimic the myriad synapses and connections of our actual brain cells. Recent scientific research supports growing evidence that the Mind Map is the natural manifestation of the human brain's thinking processes, and that we actually all think in internal Mind Maps!

INTERNAL MIND MAPS

In 2014, the Nobel Prize in Physiology or Medicine was divided, one half awarded to John O'Keefe and the other half jointly to May-Britt Moser and Edvard I. Moser for their findings in the field of cognitive neuroscience, and specifically their research into grid cells. These specialized brain cells work with place cells and the brain's hippocampus to create a mental representation of a person's location in their environment. Not only do they help an individual form a mental map of their surroundings, acting as a sort of inner GPS, but the evidence suggests that grid cells could play a role in the formation of episodic memories in the hippocampus, a region of the brain critical to learning and memory.

The dendrites and synapses of brain cells combine to create a form of internal Mind Map, both making sense of a situation and enabling information to be retained and recalled at a later date.

Discoveries like this never cease to amaze and delight me. When, in the 1960s, I began my research into how we think, some aspects of science were still in their relative infancy. Brain cells, for example, seemed to be like little more than dots under a microscope – tiny dust motes floating about among other particles. However, as neuroscience improved, to everyone's surprise it became clear that these dots had legs. It took the invention of the electron microscope to reveal the brain cell in its full glory, with a nucleus, branch-like dendrites, synapses and axon terminals.

The revelation struck me as a miracle in other ways, as it confirmed the validity and organic nature of the thinking tool that I had been working on in conjunction with these discoveries: the structure of the Mind Map. A good Mind Map resembles the expanded form of a brain cell.

Just as the mathematics of a brain cell lurch toward infinity, so the Mind Map is a thinking tool with the potential to expand toward the reaches of infinity.

The discovery of the brain cell's true nature seemed like a wonderful example of synchronicity. Likewise, the relatively recent Nobel Prize-winning research into grid cells confirms the fact that brain cells think in Mind Map form. I believe this revelation confirms the power of this thinking tool, and also its key relationship with memory.

That said, the relationship between Mind Maps and memory has already been scientifically proven. A paper presented by H. Toi at the International Conference on Thinking, Kuala Lumpur, in 2009, showed that Mind Mapping can help children recall words more effectively than using lists, with improvements in memory of up to 32 percent. Similarly, a study conducted by Paul Farrand, Fearzana Hussain and Enid Hennessy in 2002 demonstrated how Mind Mapping improved the long-term memory of factual information in their participants by 10 percent.

MIND MAPS ARE WHO WE ARE

Mind Maps offer the easiest way to get information into the brain as well as to take information out of it, and appear to connect with an integral part of our nature as human beings. The Hermetic saying "as above, so below" seems apt, given that Mind Maps mirror our inner and outer workings: they relate both to the ways in which we think in terms of the brain's structure, and to the ways in which our thoughts can be made manifest in the world through the ultimate thinking tool of the Mind Map.

By the time you have finished reading this book and worked your way through the exercises in it, you will be on well on the way toward Mind Mapping Mastery. Not only that, by learning to Mind Map, you could be on the path to realizing your true potential as a human being.

2

How to Mind Map

This chapter explains the Laws of
Mind Mapping, why the Laws work
and why they remain essential. You
will discover all the benefits of Mind
Mapping for everyday living, and their
key applications: at home, at work, in
education and for creativity, wellbeing
and memory. Discover how to use
Mind Maps to maximize your happiness,
fulfilment and productivity each and
every day!

Unlock the Potential of Your Brain

Unlike other types of visual tool, Mind Mapping unlocks the incredible potential of the brain by engaging the full range of cortical skills, from the rational and numerical to the imaginative and inventive. A good Mind Map provides an arena in which to brainstorm creatively using a combination of words and images. In fact, Mind Maps are better than this, as they encourage "brain blooming" through the combined powers of the imagination and association, creating the perfect conditions for a proliferation of ideas – and the more ideas you generate, the better their overall quality is likely to be. Mind Mapping will broaden the horizons of your thinking and will offer you the means to boost your mental accuracy, insight, creativity and freedom of thought.

In the decades since their first introduction, Mind Maps have been adopted by hundreds of millions of people around the world in order to maximize the efficient use of their brainpower. Their effectiveness has been confirmed by numerous scientific and psychological studies, and they have proven themselves to be a remarkably versatile tool. As we will discover in Chapter 5, a Mind Map can be used in absolutely any aspect of life where improved learning and clearer thinking will enhance performance.

Ask yourself, "How can Mind Mapping improve my life?" Now begin!

In Chapter 1, I invited you to create your own Mind Map by way of introducing you to a Mind Map's key components such as images, colours, branches and words (see page 27). As with any skill, your Mind Mapping confidence and technique will improve the more you practise. To get the most out of this chapter, I suggest you approach it as an enjoyable set of fun, practical exercises. Set aside any inhibitions or insecurities, and have a go at making lots of different colourful Mind Maps following the principles that I will lay out in more detail in the following pages.

Before we begin, I'd like to make a quick suggestion: although you will be giving your brain a vigorous workout, be kind to yourself (always!). Your Mind Maps will lead to the best results when your approach is lighthearted, colourful and interesting. Paradoxically, play is a serious business because it activates the imagination, which is one of the lynchpins of Mind Mapping. If you find yourself getting stuck or frustrated at any point, take a break and come back to your Mind Map later. (See Chapter 4, "Solution Finding", for more guidance.) Or start another one, perhaps from the quiver of Mind Maps offered in "The 99 Applications" in Chapter 5 (see page 159). Mind Mapping is most effective when undertaken in bursts of about 20 minutes.

Mind Mapping is not about "success-and-failure", "do-or-die" rigid thinking per se, and nobody is going to judge you on your results (unless you enter the World Mind Mapping Championships!). There are certain Laws that will help you get the most out of Mind Mapping and enable you to create particularly powerful Mind Maps. The notion of Laws could perhaps seem counterintuitive at first when it comes to creativity and the generation of ideas; however, these Laws are designed to support your thinking with a structure, allowing it to flourish rather than to get tangled up and flounder.

Understanding the Laws

While the Laws of Mind Mapping are deceptively simple, they are very effective. If you deviate from them, you won't create a true Mind Map. Instead, you will probably end up with one of the diagrams that we will be looking at in Chapter 3, or with something that resembles pure chaos!

The Laws of Mind Mapping

1. Always use a blank sheet of paper, placed in landscape position. Make sure the sheet is large enough to allow you to create sub-branches and sub-sub-branches.

2. Draw a picture in the centre of the paper, representing your subject, using at least three colours.

3. Use images, symbols, codes and dimension throughout your Mind Map.

4. Select keywords and write these using capital letters.

5. Place each word or image on its own branch, so that it stands by itself.

6. Radiate flowing branches out from the central image. Make the branches thicker toward the centre of the Mind Map, and thinner as they radiate outward into sub-branches.

7. Keep branches the same length as the words or images on them.

8. Use colours throughout the Mind Map, developing your own colour code in the branches.

9. Use emphasis, arrows and connecting lines to depict associations between different related topics in your Mind Map.

10. Aim for clarity in your Mind Map by positioning your branches in carefully thought-through space. Remember that the space between things is often as important as the things themselves. Imagine, for example, the space between trees in a forest: your brain negotiates these gaps to understand where you are and where you are going, rather than the trees.

DEVELOPING YOUR OWN STYLE

Following the Laws frees you up to develop your own unique "fingerprint", or rather "eyeprint", style while staying true to the essential spirit of Mind Mapping. To get to know and truly absorb the Laws of Mind Mapping, keep a copy of them handy (perhaps in the form of a Mind Map) and consult them regularly whenever you do any Mind Mapping. Within a short time they will have become second nature to you and act like the DNA of your Mind Map genes!

Take your Mind Mapping journey step by step: set your goals for your first Mind Map; then your first two Mind Maps; then your first five Mind Maps; your first ten Mind Maps; your first 25 Mind Maps; your first 50 Mind Maps … right until you reach your first 100 Mind Maps (your century!). By the time you have reached 100 Mind Maps, if you have been consulting the Laws, you will have attained a highly skilled level of Mind Mapping.

Mind Maps can sometimes become complex as they spread across the page. The Laws are designed to help improve their clarity in every respect and thereby strengthen their impact on your brain, as well as on the brains of other people. To get a better understanding of why this is so, let's examine the key elements in a little more detail, as well as some other considerations that relate to them.

How the Laws Shape a Mind Map

The easiest way to explore the effects and usefulness of the Laws is to put them into practice by creating a Mind Map. First, make sure you have completely grasped the basics of Mind Mapping by memorizing the seven steps set out in Chapter 1 (see page 28). Then you will be ready to apply the Laws to a Mind Map about a topic of your own choice. Why not trying creating one now, as you read the words on the following pages?

In Chapter 1, I used the example of Shakespeare to illustrate each of the steps as we went through them together. For this exercise, I would now like you to take a moment to reflect on the problem or subject you would like to Mind Map. (If you need inspiration, turn to the "Make Your Thoughts Visible" exercise on page 73.)

GATHER YOUR RESOURCES

Once you have chosen your theme, and before you start working on the Mind Map itself, gather any other materials, research or additional information you need, so that you have everything readily to hand.

Portrait position   **Landscape position**

For example, if you want to use a Mind Map to make notes about a certain text you are studying, make sure you have a copy of the book nearby so you can consult it as you create your Mind Map.

To prevent your Mind Map from becoming cramped, especially as it radiates out toward the margins, work on a large sheet of blank paper. It's important that the paper is plain white and doesn't feature lines or any decoration that will detract from your creative process. Always position this sheet of paper in a landscape position, as this will give you more freedom and space in which to create a Mind Map than paper placed in a portrait (vertical) position. Moreover, the information on a horizontal Mind Map is easier to absorb at a glance, as it allows you to scan the entire page in a non-linear fashion, radiating from the centre, rather than reading the page left to right, left to right, left to right – like watching tennis, getting a stiff neck – and top to bottom in the way that you usually tackle a text.

Place the paper on a flat or raised surface in front of you or, if you like, pin it to the wall and work standing up. A raised surface such as an architect's drawing board will improve your posture and give you a better perspective. Alternatively, Mind Map seated on the floor if you find this comfortable. Some artists, such as the Portuguese-born British painter and printmaker Paula Rego, sometimes sit on the floor to paint and draw, as this seemingly childlike approach can be liberating when it comes to thinking creatively.

You can make a Mind Map in any place, in any physical position, especially if you are a yoga practitioner, a gymnast, a dancer or a little kid. You can create a Mind Map in your meditation position, for instance, as Mind Maps will help settle and balance your thoughts by synchronizing the workings of your brain's two hemispheres. Many people, especially children, make them while lying flat on their stomach on the floor, propping up their head with their hands.

But there is no need to turn yourself into a contortionist! Keep your Mind Map as upright as you can, with its branches as close to the horizontal as possible, which will make the Mind Map much easier to read and recall. As you write and draw, allow your hand to travel across the paper, rather than rotating the paper itself.

To increase the visual appeal of your Mind Map and its impact, collect a selection of coloured easy-flowing pens, ranging in thickness from thin nib to highlighter, to vary and to strengthen your Mind Map's colour coding and visual appeal to the memory. (Remember the von Restorff effect discussed in Chapter 1, page 40.)

Make your own transportable Mind Map kit of plain paper and coloured pens, and carry this with you wherever you go. This way, you will never find yourself stuck with lined paper and a blue biro.

If you are in a business meeting, you could create a draft Mind Map in black and white, and then colour it in or redraw it completely at a later stage. It is always useful, no matter how brilliant your Mind Map is, to review it soon after completing it. So colouring in a black-and-white draft is good practice. However, colour is a key element in promoting creativity, which means that if you initially create your Mind Map in black and white, you will be radically limiting your ability to generate new ideas.

CHOOSE THE CENTRAL IMAGE

When you have a subject in mind, start to draw a central image in the middle of your paper, using dimension, self-expression and at least three colours to make it visually engaging and memorable. Think about how to symbolize your subject in as interesting and as imaginative a way as possible. If a particular word is absolutely central to your Mind Map, convert the word itself into an image by using dimension and colours to enhance its visual appeal. A dynamic central image will automatically focus the eye and the brain, triggering numerous associations.

What do you want your Mind Map to reveal to you? Keep this goal in your thoughts at every step.

SET OBJECTIVES AND BASIC ORDERING IDEAS

The main categories, which radiate in branches from the central image, are known as Basic Ordering Ideas (BOIs) and constitute the core framework of a Mind Map.

A strong set of BOIs will get your Mind Map off to the best start creatively: by identifying your BOIs and ordering them in a visually meaningful way, you will be able to see more clearly how further ideas and concepts relate to the whole and fit within your Mind Map's hierarchy of ideas.

As you begin your Mind Map, consider your objectives carefully:

- **What information or knowledge do you need?**
- **Which are the most important seven categories in the topic under consideration?**
- **If this were a book, what would its chapter headings be? What lessons or themes are there?**
- **What questions do you need to ask? (Prompts such as "What?", "Where?", "Who?", "How?", "Which?", "When?" can make very useful main branches in a Mind Map.)**
- **Into which sub-categories can you divide your topic?**

Your BOIs can also address the following considerations:

- **Structure – the form of things**
- **Function – the purpose of things and what they do**
- **Properties – the characteristics of things**
- **Processes – how things work**
- **Evaluation – how beneficial things are**
- **Definitions – what things mean**
- **Classification – how things relate to each other**
- **History – the chronological sequence of events**
- **Personalities – people's roles and characters**

To get started, you could jot down the first ten words or images that spring to mind, then group these under generic headings to form your main radiating branches.

BRANCH OUT

As suggested in Chapter 1, make the branches closest to the central image thicker, to emphasize their importance to your brain, and write your Basic Ordering Ideas (BOIs) above them. Any sub-branches that sprout from a main branch will hold information that supports that particular BOI. The most general (inclusive) concepts tend to sit closer to the central image, while the less general (more exclusive or specific) concepts appear on the sub-branches, further away from the Mind Map's centre.

If your Mind Map is still at an exploratory stage, you could well discover that some of the peripheral ideas turn out to be more important than those you initially placed toward the centre. When this happens, simply thicken up the outer branches where necessary, thereby adding another layer of interest to your Mind Map.

Make all the branches reach out in an organic, wave-like, flowing manner to enhance their visual appeal. In addition to this, if you make your branches curve and radiate organically, each one will have a unique shape which can then be further used to activate your recall of the information held within that branch.

EXPRESS YOURSELF THROUGH IMAGES

To get maximum visual impact and creative inspiration out of Mind Mapping, and have fun in the process, use images wherever possible (as with words, each of these should nestle into its own branch). Don't worry if you hated art class at school; no one is going to be judging your artistic ability. The images on your Mind Map absolutely *don't* have to be masterpieces: quick descriptive sketches, drawings, symbols and doodles all work well!. In fact, you definitely don't want to get bogged down in creating the perfect image; Mind Mapping is all about getting ideas down on paper quickly, so think of your illustrations as a form of shorthand to represent the essence of your deepest thinking.

Whereas linear note-taking uses the three basic skills of linear patterning, symbols and analysis, image making engages a wide range of cortical skills, from imagination, logic and spatial awareness to the use of colour, form, line dimension and visual patterning.

Using imagery in Mind Maps has another, wider benefit: it will help improve your everyday powers of visual perception. Whatever your level of artistry, any attempt at drawing will encourage you to focus more strongly on real life for inspiration, and you will become more aware of the world around you.

Finally, not only does a Mind Map use images; it is an image itself! A Mind Map is much easier to picture in your mind's eye than a passage of text. A study into image recognition, carried out by Professor Ralph Haber in

1970, found that humans have an almost photographic memory when it comes to the recognition of pictures, making images an excellent memory aid. Incredibly, Haber found that the average human, when shown 10,000 photographs, can remember more than 98 percent of them.

Just imagine that when you have completed your first 100 Mind Maps, you will most likely remember 100 out of 100 of them – that's 100 percent recall. Now imagine your first 1,000 Mind Maps! And *now* imagine completing 10,000 Mind Maps for 10,000 books you've studied: even if you can recall only 98 percent of them, how incredible would that be? Mind Mapping offers a relatively easy way to become a genius among geniuses! Your first 100 Mind Maps will be a battalion of soldiers against the bastion of ignorance.

Make your images as clear as possible. The greater the clarity in your Mind Map, the more elegant, graceful and attractive it will appear. A clear image will lead to a clear response. Clarity will cleanse the lenses of your eyes and will help you to see the world more like a child or an artist does. Your powers of perception will increase.

PLAY WITH WORDS

For clarity, impact and freedom, remember to use only one keyword on each branch of your Mind Map. A single keyword is a lot easier to remember than a phrase and will lodge in the memory. Like a pebble dropped in a pool, it will ripple out and trigger lots of different associations, thereby stimulating your thinking. Moreover, by focusing on one word per branch, you are forced to deliberate about precisely which word best represents your idea. This means actively engaging your powers of discrimination and analysis; and it is often a process that requires a degree of focus that is lacking in linear note-taking, which by comparison can be a much more passive and unproductive practice.

A keyword should always sit on a branch of the same length. This will allow you to place a number of words in close proximity to each other in your Mind Map, thereby encouraging you to find even more associations as the words "bounce" off each other. It will also make your Mind Map appear less cluttered and allow you to include more information in it.

Write the words in capitals to give them definition and to make it easier for your mind to visualize them. Keeping your Mind Map's hierarchy of ideas in mind, you can use upper and lower case letters in the sub-branches to show the relative importance of words on your Mind Map.

To make the most important elements in your Mind Map stand out and become easy to remember, write any words associated with them in

THREE DIMENSIONS

DEVELOP SYNAESTHESIA

The word "synaesthesia" refers to a perceptual phenomenon in which a reaction is provoked in a sense or a part of the body through the stimulation of another sense or body part. For example, a person with synaesthesia might associate each day of the week with a different colour and texture: Tuesdays might be blue with the texture of deep-pile carpet, while Sundays could be yellow with the texture of bubbles.

Synaesthesia is often described as a mental disorder that causes people to become confused by their sensory perceptions. I would argue that this attitude is mistaken, as well-organized synaesthesia can actually increase the powers of the brain. A Mind Map can be considered an organized synaesthetic thinking tool. In a way, it is a physical and mental manifestation of the power of association. So, let's dispel any fears about this. Use synaesthesia when Mind Mapping by engaging all five senses in your words and images: sight, smell, hearing, taste and touch. Also think about the power of movement, which can be suggested through the organic form of the branches, and consider in what other ways this can be made manifest in a Mind Map.

BECOME A CODE MAKER

We have already seen how colour is one of the most powerful tools for enhancing memory and creativity. To make your use of colour have even more impact, create your own colour codes by matching specific colours to your BOIs. A carefully considered use of colour codes will help you access the information in your Mind Map more quickly, improve your memory of it, and increase the number and range of your creative ideas.

Imagine you are, for example, creating a Mind Map of *Wu Xing*, the five traditional elements in Chinese philosophy. Keeping the most suitable colours in mind, you would decide to colour the main branch for Wood in green, Fire in orange, Earth in brown, Metal in silver and Water in blue.

In addition to using colour codes in your main branches, you can create other codes to forge instant connections between different areas of your Mind Map. These codes could be quite simple and take the form of crosses and ticks, for example; or underlines and shapes such as circles, triangles and squares placed carefully around your Mind Map; or they could be more elaborate symbols – even shown in 3D. Think of the traditional footnote symbols used in typography as a prototype of the sorts of symbol you could invent. And remember the Major System that I mentioned briefly in the Introduction, which uses a code to convert numbers into sounds and then words.

Like footnote symbols, you can use codes to link source material such as biographical references to your Mind Map, or to represent particular elements such as any names, dates or events that crop up frequently in your notes. Whichever codes you create, they will help reinforce the categorization and hierarchy of your ideas in the Mind Map.

The more visually exciting your Mind Map, the better your results will be.

MAKE CONNECTIONS

Like codes, connecting branches and relationship arrows can be used to link up separate areas and branches on a Mind Map, showing how seemingly different concepts relate to each other. In this way, branches and arrows also help your brain create connections between ideas. In keeping with a Mind Map's use of imagery, connecting branches can take the form of curves, circles, loops and chains or any other shapes that appeal to your imagination.

Relationship arrows will automatically direct your eye to connect one part of a Mind Map with another; in this way, they encourage your mind to follow your gaze and thereby give spatial direction to your thoughts, promoting divergent and highly creative thinking. Like connecting branches, arrows can vary in size, form and dimension. They can also be multi-headed, linking a number of different branches.

USE BOUNDARIES AND CHUNKING

I invented Brain Pattern Notes in the 1950s and 1960s as a precursor to the fully fledged Mind Map. They featured in my BBC TV series *Use Your Head*. Although Brain Pattern Notes relied on words rather than images, they used branches and colour: in them, I instinctively surrounded separate branches and their sub-branches with colourful boundaries. Those boundaries could take the form of a wavy line or a cloud-like bubble, and would enclose a set of ideas associated with a specific topic in a way that made them easy to remember and to communicate to others.

Little did I know it at the time, but this technique is similar to chunking, which is a well-known mnemonic technique first described by the American psychologist George Armitage Miller (1920–2012) in 1956. The term came from Miller's famous paper "The Magical Number Seven, Plus or Minus Two", in which he explained how the short-term memory can only store seven items of information efficiently. Miller then described how a technique such as chunking can be used to extend memory span.

As I developed the Mind Map, I saw how chunking could play a useful role in certain circumstances. In Mind Mapping, the outline of a boundary creates a unique shape of its own, making it memorable in its own right, as well as grouping information in a way that suits the workings of the short-term memory. Boundaries and chunking can be especially helpful when creating intricate Mind Maps that cover a variety of topics with many different levels of information.

However, boundaries and chunking should be applied sensitively to Mind Maps, as there is a delicate balance at work. If a Mind Map is still a work in progress, every extending branch needs to be "open" and free to make new connections. If a branch is outlined with a boundary too soon, the Mind Mapper will potentially place themselves in a restrictive prison.

Ensure that you never confine your thinking to a linear prison. A good Mind Mapper remains free.

Make Your Thoughts Visible

Feeling stuck? Choose one of these topics as your central concept:

happiness   **peace**   **work**   **success**

Now that you have your Mind Map starter kit, it is time to practise creating Mind Maps. The more you can do, the better! Keep referring to the Laws as you go.

Once you have completed your Mind Map, take a good look at it. What do you like about it? What needs a little more attention? Mind Map your own responses and reactions.

Now, choose another subject and start again.

GIVE YOURSELF SPACE TO BREATHE

We have seen how the size of a word or an image is used to denote its importance in a Mind Map's hierarchy.

The larger an item, the greater its visual impact and the more likely you will be to recall it.

The space between elements in a Mind Map can be as important as the items themselves. The right amount of space around each item will give your Mind Map clarity and structure, and make it more visually appealing – which in turn means that you are more likely to absorb the information in it.

73

Development of a Mind Mapper

There are three stages in the careers of most successful Mind Mappers:

Acceptance: Before you start Mind Mapping, set aside any preconceptions you have about your intelligence, your imagination or your artistic skill. Follow the Laws of Mind Mapping until you become completely familiar with them. You will discover even more about the importance of images and colour by studying the works of artists such as Leonardo da Vinci and Lorraine Gill, who influenced the development of Mind Mapping.

Application: Once you have understood the Laws, apply them by creating as many Mind Maps as you can. Use Mind Maps whenever you need to take notes, for example, or if you need to make decisions or acquire a new skill. You will find a range of practical applications suggested in this chapter. Have a go at these, and think of other ways in which Mind Mapping will enhance and enrich your own life.

Adaptation: With time, you will develop a personal Mind Mapping style. Once you have created hundreds of Mind Maps, you will be ready to experiment by adapting the Mind Map form, taking it to the next level.

Journalling

Keep a working Mind Map journal to make Mind Maps part of your everyday life, perhaps using an exercise book or a ring binder. Just make sure that the paper in it is blank and unlined so that your brain is free to think creatively, in a non-linear and uninhibited way. Put your first Mind Map in pride of place on the first page of your journal. (Glue the Mind Maps into your journal if necessary.) You can use a Mind Map journal productively alongside Mind Mapping diaries, schedules and planners (see Chapter 5, page 164). A journal will allow you to see how your skill at Mind Mapping improves with time. It will provide a storehouse for your ideas, so that you can see at a glance how your thinking is evolving. And it will be a handy resource to dip into whenever you need inspiration.

Key Applications of Mind Maps

When I originally developed the Mind Map, I didn't realize at first quite how adaptable this thinking tool is. To begin with, I was intent on finding a harmonic way to externalize thoughts – to materialize on the outside what lay inside the workings of the brain. As I've mentioned, this took some decades to achieve and in the process an architecture of thinking emerged that with time evolved into the Mind Map. When I had refined the Mind Map, my fascination with the art of memory remained at the fore, and I used Mind Mapping mainly as a mnemonic device. A breakthrough came when my brother, Professor Barry Buzan, challenged me to revisit my entire approach to Mind Mapping. He asked me why I had only developed the Mind Map for the purposes of memory, rather than for other forms of thinking such as creativity. At first, I dismissed his suggestion. But I slept on it, and the next day I realized my brother was right! Mind Maps can naturally be applied to all areas of life.

MIND MAP THE KEY APPLICATIONS OF MIND MAPPING!

Later in this chapter, we will be looking in more detail at the varied and exciting ways in which Mind Mapping can be used. Before zooming in on the detail, let's concentrate on some of the key applications of Mind Mapping – and what better way to do this than through a Mind Map!

Step 1

To Mind Map the six major applications of Mind Maps, begin with the central image. In this central image, the word "APPLICATIONS" is surrounded by the outline of a key to make the word itself more memorable.

Step 2

A branch grows from the central image. In this Mind Map, it takes the label "HOME" and is coloured orange (for hearth and home). The main branch starts to grow sub-branches. HOME, for example, is associated with love, family, friends and pastimes.

Step 3

Five more main branches follow for WORK, EDUCATION, CREATIVITY, WELLBEING and MEMORY. Some of these have small relevant symbols beside them.

Step 4

These main branches also start to grow sub-branches. EDUCATION, for example, is associated with school, university, studies and exams.

1

2

3

4

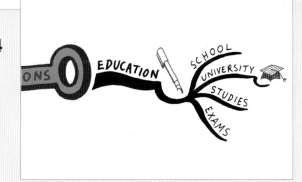

5

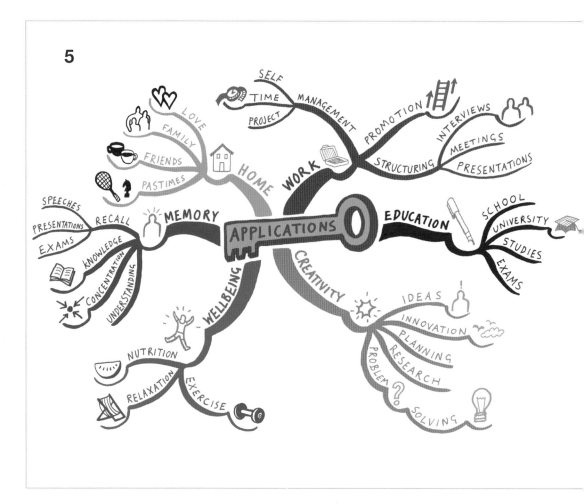

Step 5

The completed Mind Map follows the Laws with a single word sitting on each branch, accompanied by lots of fun and memorable images.

While this Mind Map looks at the six key applications for Mind Mapping, think about the six aspects YOU would choose if you were to make a Mind Map representing the key areas in your own life.

Think of this Mind Map about key applications as an embryonic Mind Map with which to explore the incredible universe of your life. These first six applications are planets and your Mind Map is a spacecraft that will enable you to visit each of the six landing points in turn. Once one of them has been explored or completed – perhaps when you have achieved a goal or become a champion in your field – Mind Mapping will help you travel on to discover new experiences and meet new challenges.

You can use a Mind Map for every aspect of your life: business or leisure, study or personal development. You could, for example, Mind Map the best conversations you've ever had, or create a Mind Map for your dreams, then use the Mind Map to turn those dreams into stories or poems.

The next pages explore each of the fundamental applications of Mind Maps – home, work, education, creativity, wellbeing and memory – in each case suggesting lots of great ways in which you can use Mind Mapping to achieve your goals in those areas of life. I have included some sample Mind Maps to act as inspiration and a possible starting point, but of course, as each person's Mind Maps are unique to them, your own Mind Maps will probably end up looking quite different. More advanced usages of Mind Maps for each of their key applications are suggested throughout Chapter 5.

KEY MIND MAP APPLICATION 1: HOME

For many of us, the old saying is true: home is where the heart is. Home provides a refuge from the world and a place in which to express our individuality and enjoy some of our closest relationships. It is both a safe haven and the equivalent of an alchemist's crucible – where we create important memories and experience life-changing milestones such as birth, childhood, marriage, parenthood and retirement. It's also the place where we nurture our dreams and chase our personal ambitions – and have fun and throw parties!

Achieve a Personal Goal

Take a moment to reflect on the areas in your daily life that are most important to you. Now think about what goals you would like to achieve. The Mind Map *opposite* is all about training for a marathon, but its underlying principles could be adapted to help you achieve any personal goal. The Basic Ordering Ideas (BOIs) reflect a long-distance runner's key concerns: training, nutrition, equipment, motivation and obstacles. Using this Mind Map as inspiration, make a Mind Map for a goal of your own.

Draw a central image that represents what you want to achieve. Next, reflect on this central image and create BOI branches that relate to it. These could relate to the practical steps you need to take and things you need to acquire, whether that's equipment to buy or something more intangible, such as courage or perseverance. Motivation is an important branch, as keeping going is crucial to any long-term goal. You can explore all the benefits you will gain from success, whether they relate to your health, finances or self-esteem, and note down who or what will support you in your endeavour. You might want another branch about obstacles, as facing up to all the possible obstacles is a good starting point for dealing with them. Your sub-branches will delve deeper into these themes, to pin down

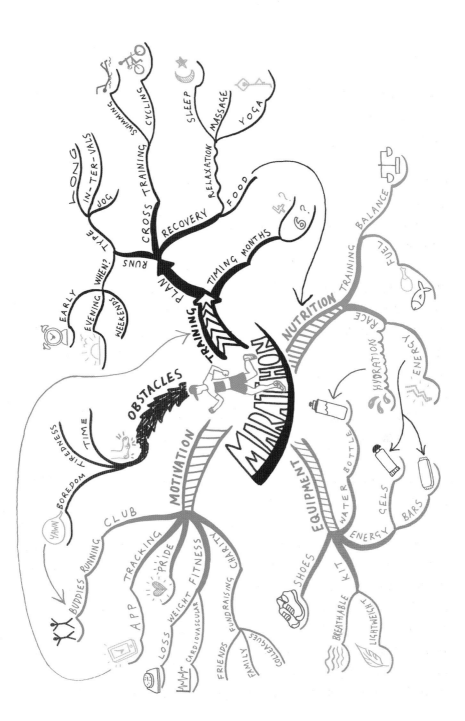

details such as the length of time you need to reach your goal, and exactly what you need to do to get there. You can explore the individual stages of your journey as fully as you need in this Mind Map, or perhaps create more Mind Maps to explore each step further.

If you have a tendency to put other peoples' needs ahead of your own, you are likely to find goal-setting Mind Mapping especially helpful. Perhaps you'd love to run a marathon but you always end up being too busy rushing around on behalf of others – getting the kids to football matches, picking up your partner from the gym – to do any exercise of your own at all (never mind training for a marathon!). If so, creating a Mind Map is a great way to ensure your own goal becomes a priority in the everyday routine of you and your family. Hang your finished Mind Map on the wall to remind you and everyone else of your dream ambition, and make sure striving to achieve it really does become part of your daily life.

Plan Your Week

Setting aside your big life goals for a moment, what do you need to achieve this week? How about tomorrow or even later on today?

Mind Maps make great personal organizers and planners. Rather than clicking on individual dates on a computer screen, leafing through diary pages or flicking endlessly through a calendar, a Mind Map of your weekly activities enables you to digest in one go what lies ahead. Forewarned is forearmed, and when you can you see at a glance what the week holds, you will be prepared and know how to allocate your time and energy most productively.

For your central image, choose a symbol that represents your thoughts about the week, or the most important aspect of it. Alternatively, you could simply draw a picture of your home, or represent the date in some way,

WEEK 26

TUESDAY
WORK
10 A.M. MEETING
LUNCH W/BOSS
4 P.M. OPTICIAN
MIA PLAYDATE

WEDNESDAY
WORK
2 P.M. PRESENTATION
GYMNASTICS
JORDON
RING MUM

THURSDAY
6 A.M. PILATES
WORK TRAINING
MIKE LUNCH

MONDAY
MIA
FOOTBALL
JORDON
GUITAR
WORK
RESEARCH PRESENTATION
SATURDAY TICKETS
RESTAURANT
BABYSITTER
BOOK

FRIDAY
OFF DAY
FOOD SHOPPING
BEACH
CARD PRESENT
CHOCOLATE?
CD? PRESENT

SATURDAY
9 P.M. GIG
7 P.M. RESTAURANT
2 P.M. CYCLING JORDON
10 A.M. HAIRDRESSER

SUNDAY
LUNCH
CHICKEN
SALAD
MERINGUE
KIDS
P.M. HOMEWORK
11 A.M. SWIMMING

such as with a 3D version of "Week XX" (it's Week 26 in our example). Moving clockwise around the central image, use different colours to create seven main branches, one for each day of the week. Write the day above the branch, then fill the sub-branches with things you would like to remember, or scheduled activities. Use connecting arrows to link similar activities on different days, or add some chunking if there is a set of activities that is particularly important on one of the days.

In the example on page 83, the Mind Mapper is planning a wonderful wedding anniversary celebration on Saturday night, so the central images include a loving couple, as well as an excited child (there are lots of play dates happening that week too). Planning the celebrations involves Mind Mapping a reminder on Monday to book a restaurant and tickets to see a band, as well as the all-important babysitter. The gifts and the card will be taken care of on Friday – with Mind Mapping there's no danger of getting into trouble over a forgotten anniversary or birthday! All the other key events of the week are Mind Mapped too, from meetings and a presentation at work to children's activities to exercise sessions.

You may find it helpful to use your weekly Mind Map alongside Mind Mapping planners and schedulers (see Chapter 5, page 164), as this will allow you to zoom in on the details of individual days as well as gain an overview of longer periods of time. That way, you will be able to look ahead and enjoy a degree of control over your schedule, avoid clashes and any potentially unpleasant surprises, making sure you maintain a healthy and rewarding balance of work, rest and play.

PLAN TOGETHER

If you share your home with other people, whether that's family or housemates, why not create a joint weekly planner Mind Map for all your activities? Many of us will have experienced the disagreements and rows that can flare up when there are conflicting activities enjoyed by different members of the household, or when individuals don't seem to be pulling their weight and taking on their fair share of the housework or other tasks. Another problem for many households lies in the way in which the different members simply don't know what the others are up to when they are not all together. The good news is that a Mind Map can remedy this and change everybody's behaviour for the better by making household members more appreciative of each other as they begin to understand just how busy everybody else is, or simply by making sure that everybody takes their turn to take out the trash and do the washing up!

Like a personal weekly planner Mind Map, a joint planner will include branches for each day of the week ahead, with sub-branches showing all the different activities – and, importantly, chores! – that are scheduled to take place on any one day. You can also use a Mind Map like this to inspire everyone to stick to their chosen goal, whether that's practising guitar for 20 minutes every day or going for a run three times a week. Stick your joint planner to the fridge or somewhere else where everyone can see it and it can't be ignored.

Mind Mapping households are happier and healthier – and give each other more breaks!

Plan a Kids' Party

Who doesn't enjoy a good party? Planning a party, however, can be quite another matter – especially a children's party, where expectations appear to have rocketed in recent years. Long gone are the days when you could just feed the little darlings some jelly and ice cream, and expect them to entertain themselves for a couple of hours. Today, throwing a kid's birthday party can be a bit like organizing a military manoeuvre, covering all the

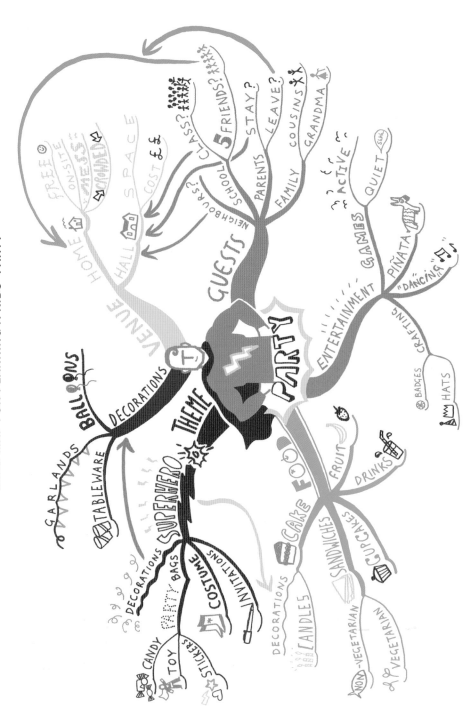

bases and preparing for every eventuality. Happily, the Mind Map is on hand to help. In this Mind Map, I've used the example of a children's birthday party with a superhero theme, but you can of course use any theme you like – or leave out the children completely, if you wish!

The core logistics of most parties are the same for children and adults: once you've set the date, you need to choose a theme (if you want one) and a venue, setting considerations such as cost, space and transport against each other. Then draw up your guest list and plan the entertainment, the food and drinks and the decorations, exploring these on the main branches and sub-branches of your Mind Map. If the party is going to include any special features, such as games, swimming or a magician, include these in your Mind Map too. You could also use one of the branches to explore how your party will reflect the theme, perhaps through costumes, decorations and the small gifts that the children get to take home. With an exciting topic such as a kid's party, you can really have fun creating your Mind Map, especially if there is a theme involved.

Find the Perfect Gift

You are well ahead with the party planning, so now you have plenty of time to buy gifts. A Mind Map is a great way to record the likes and dislikes of your family and friends when it comes to buying presents. If you have ever found yourself wandering in a daze around a department store clutching a solitary pair of socks or a shopping basket crammed with potential gifts, and no idea whom to give them to, you will likely find a Mind Map that organizes your ideas very handy.

To create your own gift-finding Mind Map, draw an inspiring central image in the centre of a horizontal sheet of paper. This could be a wrapped-up parcel with a bow on top, or a star bursting out of a box, or something wild like a unicorn with a rainbow-coloured horn to symbolize wishes coming true.

Use your imagination to make your central image interesting and eye-catching to capture the spirit of gift giving.

Now create colour-coded main branches for each of the people on your shopping list. Create sub-branches for their likes and dislikes. Use symbols as well as words to illustrate these. Fill your sub-branches with fun images that relate to the intended recipient of the gift.

Next, create sub-sub-branches to push your imagination and inventiveness on to the next level. In a perfect world, what would you buy that person if money were no object? Or if there were no considerations of geography to take into account, or any other obstacles? Returning to reality, what would a fun (and affordable) equivalent be?

When you have completed your Mind Map, keep it in your yearly planner, where you can refer to it whenever a friend's or relative's birthday approaches. Or use it a little bit like a conventional list at Christmas time, ticking off each of the branches once the perfect present has been found for that person.

Remember: never cross out anything on a Mind Map!

Crossing out anything on a Mind Map means obliterating what you have accomplished and erasing a memory of your life; in contrast, a page full of positive ticks or smiley faces acknowledges your accomplishments. If you are using your Mind Map to buy presents or plan an event, always use a tick or another appropriate symbol when you've found the perfect gift or completed a task.

Plan a Romantic Minibreak

Have you ever fallen in love and wanted to treat your heart's desire to a wonderful surprise? Or perhaps you have been together for years, and are looking for ways to rekindle the flames of romance? What better way to celebrate or cement your relationship than by whisking your loved one off to a wonderful location for a minibreak, where you can spend quality time together … Unfortunately, like throwing a party, planning a romantic getaway can sometimes be a stressful business, and the worry of organizing it can take the spark out of the experience before you even get there. To make your time together magic rather than mayhem, use a Mind Map to plan all the details, from where to stay to how to get there to what to do.

Whether you are going to treat your loved one to a mini break complete with woodland walks, fine wines and cosying up by the fire, or dancing till dawn on an exotic beach somewhere, use a Mind Map to fine-tune the details. In the area of romance, Mind Maps can act like a magic wand, helping the enchantment of love to become stronger – and remain strong, as it means that passion and impulse are tempered with thoughtfulness and planning.

Once you return from your break, if everything has gone well you could keep your Mind Map as a precious memento. If, on the other hand, things haven't gone smoothly, perhaps for reasons beyond your control, you could keep the Mind Map as a handy reminder about what to do differently next time (which might even mean going away with another person …).

Improve a Difficult Relationship

Sometimes, despite the best of intentions, a relationship hits the rocks. The trouble might not always occur in a relationship with a romantic partner, but could just as easily be with a parent, a sibling, a colleague or a friend. Whoever is the source of your unhappiness, relationship difficulties can be a devastating experience and it can be very difficult to know how to make

MIND MAP FOR IMPROVING A DIFFICULT RELATIONSHIP

things better or to repair any damage. If you are experiencing problems in a relationship, a Mind Map can help you find a sense of perspective and a way forward; it could help you understand the other person's position and spot where you can compromise. (See also Chapter 5, page 169, for a more advanced approach to conflict resolution.)

In a Mind Map like this, the idea is not to close down your thinking, to confirm any prejudices you could be harbouring, or to entrench your position, but to remain true to the principles of Radiant Thinking – and to allow your ideas to radiate out accordingly. To that end, I would advise you to use neutral or positive terms wherever possible in your Mind Map. In my example *opposite*, the Mind Mapper has a problem with his brother, Dan. He's chosen a central image of a bike to represent the positive childhood memories he has of going cycling with Dan. The first branch explores the feelings that bubble up at the thought of Dan, both negative and positive. The second branch delves into specifics of what the Mind Mapper doesn't like about Dan, while the third branch moves on to look in more detail at the Mind Mapper's own response to Dan; doing this, he begins to understand how he can respond to Dan in a better way. The fourth branch, which ends up being the biggest branch, looks at all the things that the Mind Mapper loves about his brother, and the final branch explores who he could turn to support his attempts at reconciling. Interestingly, the girlfriend who was initially perceived as a problem (one of the reasons Dan is unavailable) becomes a potential source of help on this branch.

Make your Mind Map honest, open and balanced. Work through your emotions, yet remain receptive: for every potential negative, include a positive. If you find the process upsetting, take a break and come back to the Mind Map when you feel calmer. When you return to it, you may well find that it already reveals all sorts of possibilities that will help you find a way out of this challenging situation.

KEY MIND MAP APPLICATION 2: WORK

According to recent statistics, the average Briton will spend the equivalent of 12 full years at work during his or her lifetime. What's more, researchers at London Metropolitan University have found that four years of this period will be spent talking on the phone. A study by *Management Today* claims that workers in the public sector are likely to spend nearly two years of their working life in meetings, and around six months of this time will be wasted on needless minutiae and pointless discussions …

In the face of such discouraging facts, how can we make our working lives more productive and enjoyable? With Mind Maps of course!

Whether you are creating a Mind Map for research work or for project management, approach it in the spirit of a game, rather than as a chore, to ensure a creative win–win outcome!

The following pages explore some key uses of Mind Maps in a business environment, from time management to research to report writing. See also Chapter 5 for more advanced applications of Mind Mapping in the workplace and elsewhere.

Time Management

Mind Mapping is a multitask tool so it's ideal for helping you to multitask! We have already seen how useful a Mind Map can be for planning your week (page 82). Do you find yourself getting so caught up in the day-to-day demands of work that you never get a chance to plan and prioritize? Creating a work-focused Mind Map at the start of the working week, or perhaps at the end of the preceding one, is a great way of forcing yourself to stop and reassess your priorities. A Mind Map for time management could be structured around the days of the week, highlighting deadlines and important events, or perhaps the BOIs could reflect the different projects you are working on, with sub-branches exploring the key priorities for each project over the week to come. It may feel counter-intuitive to stop work in order to create a Mind Map, but time spent managing your time will create even more time in the long run!

Research a Topic

If you work in an office environment, the chances are you will have to carry out some research at some point. This could be into sales performance, new markets to explore, or innovative and money-saving approaches to existing tasks.

When using a Mind Map to research a topic, create a central image that defines the subject succinctly and positively. The first of your main branches could represent the approach or angle you intend to take, while the second may list the types of information you will need to research, such as evidence, opinion, hard facts, and other existing research and analyses. A third branch could relate to your sources, with sub-branches for primary and secondary sources. Your fourth branch would then be for ways you can assess your material, while a fifth branch looked at how best to organize your information and findings. Perhaps dedicate a sixth branch to the best ways in which to present your research to maximize its impact.

The sub-branches would look at these main areas in more detail. As you fill them in, you may be surprised by the ideas that come up – don't censor them. Mind Mapping is great for "thinking outside the box". Don't be afraid to leave sub-branches empty at times; this will encourage you to come up with creative solutions to fill the gaps.

Write an Annual Report

In the Mind Map example *opposite*, you are faced with the daunting task of creating an annual report. While making your accounts public in an annual report may be a legal requirement, this is also an opportunity to showcase your business and its successes over the last year in order to attract investors and customers, and really make your enterprise stand out in the marketplace.

Your central image could be one that encapsulates the company vision, to help you keep it to the forefront of your mind. If you are an organic juice manufacturer, as in the example in this book, you might want to sketch a trendy bottle surrounded by fruit.

Now work through the structure of your report, allocating a branch for each element. As you work, you'll probably find that creative solutions and unusual approaches spring to mind. For example, perhaps the CEO could be filmed delivering the introduction and a link to this recording embedded in the online version of the document. One branch could explore the industry overview and the opportunities and challenges recent changes have presented to your company. The next branch could then delve into the report's next section: a recap of business objectives, especially with regard to financial targets, the need to stay ahead of the market in terms of design and also offer great customer service.

Then move onto achievements – this is an important branch so be creative with your Mind Map design. One branch will remind you of the financial details you need to include, and you can use another one to explore possible conclusions. Finally, take a branch or two to think about ideas for the design of the document (especially important if you are work in a creative or fashionable industry) and the presentation itself, if the report is going to be delivered as part of an event.

MIND MAP FOR WRITING AN ANNUAL REPORT

A Journey on the Magic Carpet of Mind Mapping

Excellent tools for planning and memorization, Mind Maps have an especially strong affinity with the spheres of work and education, making these aspects of our lives much more rewarding and pleasurable, as demonstrated by the story of Sri Lankan-born Dr Dilip Abayasekara.

Today, Dilip is in demand as a professional speaker, communications trainer and author whose books include *The Path of the Genie: Your Journey to Your Heart's Desire*. He is also a former International President of Toastmasters International, a worldwide non-profit educational organization that empowers individuals to become effective communicators and leaders. Yet Dilip started his career as a scientist. On his way to work one day, he started listening to a tape recording about Mind Mapping and became hungry to learn more. He takes up his story:

> I started to Mind Map and discovered the power of it from my very first attempt. At that time, I was a scientist. I applied Mind Mapping to my work, using it to outline my reports from my lab notebook, and to analyse technical issues, spot patterns, gain insights and organize data. The discovery of the potential applications of Mind Mapping was a mind-blowing and mind-liberating experience as I applied Mind Mapping to anything and everything! I also discovered that if you Mind Map your thoughts, you can think better! I was so excited about the power of this tool, I taught it to my wife and my two children.

I went on to have a career transition from being a scientist into being a speech coach and trainer, a college professor and a pastor (all of which I currently do). The one indispensable tool that is common to all of these exciting ventures is Mind Mapping. I have taught hundreds of professionals and pastors how to Mind Map.

I was (and still am) an avid speaker and a member of Toastmasters, so it was quite natural to apply Mind Mapping to speech preparation. Gone were the days when I laboured over a speech, writing every sentence in linear form! I discovered that not only was speech preparation more fun, I generated more ideas, saved more time, and had the Mind Map so etched in my mind that I did not need to refer to notes when I delivered the speech! In fact, I recall that one day when I was driving to a Toastmasters' club meeting located an hour away, I asked my pre-teen daughter to Mind Map a speech that I dictated to her as I drove. It was from my daughter's Mind Map that I delivered my speech that evening!

If anyone ever doubts their capacity to think intelligently and creatively, and have fun doing it, I offer one solution – stop dragging your mental feet on the road of life; jump on to the magic carpet of Mind Mapping! It is a tool for mental liberation and a path to the joy of discovering one's limitless capacity to think, create and revel in using what we too often take for granted – the mind!

If you are involved in academia or education, you could adapt an annual report-style Mind Map for giving lectures, presenting papers or essay writing (see Essay Planning, page 102).

**Limit your Mind Mapping
to bursts of 20 minutes
to keep your brain relaxed
and your thinking fresh.**

Great Project Management

Whether you are organizing a conference, launching a new product range or putting on a school play, project management is potentially a complicated and time-consuming process. It typically involves a number of stages, from the generation of ideas, to planning, delegation, allocating resources, steering and producing the finished result. A Mind Map can offer valuable help at every stage of project management.

To make sure yours is effective, use a sheet of paper that is large enough to encompass all the steps you need to take, or use mini Mind Maps where necessary (see Chapter 4, page 142). Keep an open mind at every point in the procedure, assessing the potential of every piece of new input. Make sure that every significant task or consideration in the project is allocated a major branch of its own. When tasks need to be addressed urgently, emphasize the words and images that relate to them with a highlighter pen. As soon as they have been completed, mark them off with a satisfying tick.

For an advanced Mind Map on project management, see the version on page 105 that Polish entrepreneur Marek Kasperski created for his students, which includes branches for goals, schedule, tasks, milestones, quality, budget, calendar, reporting, resources, tracking and bringing the project to a close. You can select and adapt the BOIs to suit your own project.

KEY MIND MAP APPLICATION 3: EDUCATION

I believe every child on this planet should be taught how to Mind Map as part of their basic right to a rounded education. Experience and studies have shown how Mind Maps can help young children and students of all ages improve their levels of concentration and comprehension, memorize information more easily and prepare confidently for exams.

Like any practice, it's good to start young if you want to achieve perfection. (Think of those fledgling violinists who graduate from the Yehudi Menuhin School and go on to become superstars like Nigel Kennedy and Nicola Benedetti.) I have mentioned how my Mind Mapping adventures began when I was a student, and today I receive stories from teachers and students all over the world from who have discovered the benefits of this incredible thinking tool.

But don't just take my word for it …

Revision

As will be clear by now, Mind Maps are incredibly effective revision aids, breaking down lengthy texts into easily digested nuggets of information. At some point during our education, many of us will have studied the works of great authors and thinkers, and then had to memorize enough about them in order to answer questions under exam conditions. In Chapter 1, we looked at Shakespeare as a general example of how to make a Mind Map. Now let's focus on one of his best-known works – the tragedy *Macbeth*.

According to superstition, *Macbeth* is said to be a cursed play, and actors believe it is unlucky to say its name in the theatre. Instead, they use the euphemism "the Scottish Play". At the heart of the play is the character of Macbeth, a warrior hero whose private ambitions and excessive pride lead to his downfall. A Mind Map exploring the figure of Macbeth would use a depiction of him as its central image. As I have stressed before, you mustn't worry about your artistic skills, or feel inhibited in any way, when you are creating images for your Mind Map.

A simple sketch works just as well as a detailed drawing for the central image, so long as it is colourful, full of energy and encapsulates the theme for you.

One of the main features about Macbeth is his ambition, so this is the word placed on the first main branch in this Mind Map. The branch ends in an arrow to symbolize his rocketing aspirations. The rest of the main branches relate to Macbeth's other dominant personality traits, including his courage on the battlefield, his pangs of conscience, and the way he changes from being a hero into a monster eaten up by ambition.

The Mind Map starts to sprout sub-branches to show how, for example, Macbeth's ambition expresses itself in his desire to be king and to establish his own royal line. Further sub-branches are added, referring to the ways in which each of Macbeth's dominant personality traits relates to acts in the play – such as the way in which his courage transmutes into fear, and how he overcomes the qualms of his conscience to justify murder.

The completed Mind Map reflects Macbeth's transformation from hero to zero, and indicates how his fall contributes to the outcome of the play. Note how the images create a sense of energy and capture the different facets of Macbeth's character, from the jaggedy outlines of the "deviousness" branch to the strong box edging of the "courage" branch. You can take this creative approach to provide an overview of any topic of your choosing.

MACBETH

AMBITION
- MY LINE
- MURDER
- IMAGINATION
- HYSTERICS

COURAGE
- FEAR
  - HELL
  - GHOST
  - DISCOVERY!!
- OBSESSED MANLINESS
- DARES...

MAN (the)
- CONSCIENCE
  - ADMIRES DUNCAN
  - AVOIDS MACDUFF
  - GUILT
  - JUSTIFIES
  - BANQUO
  - MURDER

MONSTER
- VICTIM?
- PAWN?
- LADY MACBETH?
- DEVIOUSNESS
  - SPIES
  - PRETENCE
  - PERSUADES MURDERERS

CHANGES
- DISTRUST MURDERER
- REALIZES
- WITCHES
- BITTER GROWS
- PLANS LIST MURDER BANQUO
- FORGETS
- FEAR
- MISLED
- TOMORROW

Essay Planning

Instead of a boring, linear essay plan, use a Mind Map to structure your written work. A Mind Map will give you a useful overview of your intended approach at an early stage, helping you to identify and resolve any potential flaws in your argument before you get bogged down in it.

Create a central image that reflects the main focus of your piece, and draw main branches from this to represent your introduction, main argument and conclusion. Add a branch for your research and another for any other relevant information. You could also add branches for any key texts or figures that are relevant to your piece. Use sub-branches for themes that run through your piece and connecting arrows to develop links between the different strands in your essay. Chunking can also be a productive way to group together important themes. Be sure to use symbols and images throughout to engage your brain and your imagination.

While your Mind Map is growing, certain keywords and images can suddenly become like supernovas, bursting out from their surroundings and generating new mini Mind Maps. Keep your mind and your options open, and follow where these lead (see also Chapter 4, page 142, on the use of mini Mind Maps in solution finding).

Once you have completed a draft Mind Map and refined your argument, filling out the details of your introduction and conclusion along the way, you could find it useful to make this draft the basis of another, more "polished" Mind Map. Keep referring to both Mind Maps as you write your final piece.

The steps for writing an essay can also be adapted so that your Mind Map becomes an excellent revision aid, as in the example exploring the character of Macbeth on page 99.

A Mind Map for All Ages

I am sometimes asked whether Mind Maps can be used by people of all ages with equal success. The answer to this question is a resounding YES!

Skill in Mind Mapping is not dependent on age, sex, colour or creed; a Mind Map is a reflection of the brain's raw intelligence.

A Mind Map is a mirror of the mind's inner workings. In this way, a bright and imaginative child is just as likely to create a useful Mind Map as a CEO of many years' standing. Moreover, all children are equipped with the "kids' kit" of questions – Why? How? What? When? Where? – which act like grappling hooks to reach the peaks of knowledge. Adults would do well to adopt a childlike approach when Mind Mapping!

Let's remind ourselves of the Laws of Mind Mapping (see Chapter 2, page 60). The Laws place no emphasis on expertise or experience. In Mind Mapping, the use of colour, imagination and inventiveness confirm the natural development of artistic skill. In addition, a Mind Map is constructed from images and individual keywords rather than turns of phrase. This means that a Mind Map cuts through jargon, waffle and artifice to get to the heart of a matter in a manner that is slightly reminiscent of the way in which, for example, a young child speaks its mind.

Finally, a Mind Map relies on the power of Radiant Thinking rather than on deduction and reduction. As an open-minded thinking tool, a Mind Map charts the processes of the brain in action instead of fixating on conclusions and outcomes.

Planting a Garden of Ideas

Marek Kasperski is a Polish entrepreneur, the Online Editor of *Synapsia* magazine and a lecturer. He explains how Mind Maps inform his teaching methods, while his Mind Map shows the sort of detail that can be included in an advanced version:

A Mind Map is like a garden where ideas can grow and blossom so that others who view it may also be inspired. As a lecturer in higher education, I often need to explain difficult concepts to students of varying abilities. Not only do Mind Maps help my students understand these concepts, they make it much easier for them to revise and remember the salient points. A Mind Map excites their imagination, starts them on a journey and helps them discover new areas to explore. I encourage them to create their own Mind Maps during lectures. This often leads them to ask questions they might not otherwise have considered, which benefits the entire class.

The Mind Maps I create for my classes range from very small concept maps to large ones encompassing an entire subject. I find it's crucial to follow the Laws of Mind Mapping. My students respond to images very well, especially those who have English as a second language, as images speak a universal language. Using colour in a Mind Map is also so important. Not only is colour fun, it is essential for helping my students focus on each branch and analyse the information in it. I encourage my students to use images rather than words, or to combine the two. Many of the concepts I discuss in my Mind Maps are linked to other ideas within the Mind Map. This is of great benefit, as it assists in weaving the ideas together into a big picture.

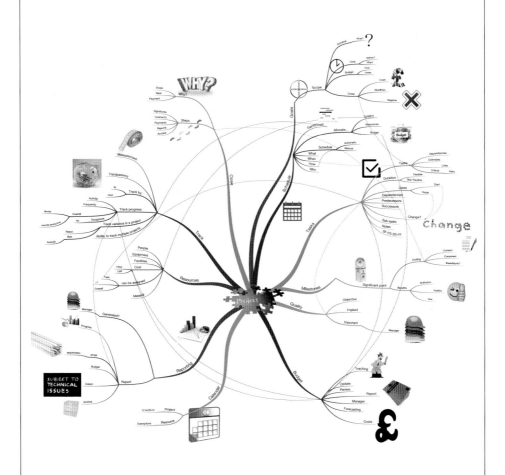

Mind Map on project management by Marek Kasperski

What Do You Want to Know?

I'm a great believer in lifelong learning. Have you ever been tempted to study a new subject or acquire a fresh skill?

Whatever your age or circumstances, you have every right to keep on pushing yourself by exercising your brain – which will help you engage with life and keep your mental faculties sharp. If you have any desire at all to nurture a talent or deepen your understanding of a particular topic, I encourage you now to explore that urge in the form of a Mind Map.

What subject interests you? Use this as the basis of your central image – and make that image colourful, imaginative and inspiring. To choose the main branches, start by addressing these questions:

- **What benefits would studying the subject have for you?**
- **What tools or study aids do you need?**
- **Where can you study?**
- **How does your subject relate to society?**
- **What outcomes do you hope to achieve from your study? Qualifications? Skills? Improved CV?**
- **What considerations or obstacles are there? How can you address these?**

Grow your sub-branches to examine these and any related points in more detail, and enliven the Mind Map with images and symbols throughout. When you have finished, take a good look at your Mind Map. What steps will you take in light of what you have discovered?

KEY MIND MAP APPLICATION 4: CREATIVITY

Creativity is like the golden egg of personal development: we all want to be more creative, yet how to climb the beanstalk, claim the treasure of creativity and bring it into our lives? Many of us may have been fed damaging myths surrounding creativity while we were growing up: that creative people are mavericks, unreliable, foolhardy and a danger to themselves and others; that they are somehow "special" and set apart from the rest of society. If this is the case, it is perhaps no surprise that we are sometimes adverse to recognizing creativity in ourselves.

A much more balanced and productive approach recognizes the many strengths of creative personalities: they tend to be pioneers, boundary pushers, inventors and intelligent risk takers. They are more often than not original, flexible, focused, colourful, driven and visionary. They are childlike without being childish.

Creative thinking isn't the prerogative of geniuses; it is simply the ability to think in original ways and to break away from the norm. Like a muscle, your creativity will grow stronger the more you exercise it. The more you practise creative thinking:

- **The easier it will be for you to come up with new ideas**
- **The more receptive you will be to fresh perspectives**
- **The more original your ideas will become**

Creativity is linked to play, another crucial part of life – the key to learning, discovery, relaxation, wellbeing and productivity. Birds and mammals all play, both in the wild and when domesticated, as do some fish, reptiles and even insects. During childhood, play changes the connections of neurons in the prefrontal cortex and helps wire the brain's executive control centre, which performs a key role in managing emotions, making plans and solving problems. Play forges the connections between brain cells and dendrites, and thereby builds up an internet of connections in a child's brain – or, to put it another way, as we discussed in Chapter 1 (see page 52), the child's own internal Mind Map.

If we are lucky, our work can sometimes feel like play. If we are not so lucky, we need to look for ways to introduce an element of play into our lives. On page 106 we saw how to use Mind Mapping to choose a new subject to study or acquire a new skill; this technique can easily be adapted for finding an enjoyable hobby or sport. It can also help you make the most of your leisure time by finding rewarding ways in which to unwind.

> **Tell me, what is it you plan to do with your one wild and precious life?**
>
> **Mary Oliver, "The Summer Day"**

Make the Most of Your Spare Time

The saying goes that "No one ever said on their deathbed, 'I wish I'd spent more time at the office'"; I'm sure the same applies to watching more TV. In the words of American poet Mary Oliver, we only have "one wild and precious life", so use a Mind Map to make the most of yours in whatever way brings you satisfaction and fulfilment.

If you find that every moment seems to be filled up with "busy-ness", a Mind Map can help you identify times of the day that you can make your own and also explore what you really want to do with them. Whether you decide to learn a new subject, take evening classes or spend your weekends in a sports hall or on a football pitch, the choice is yours.

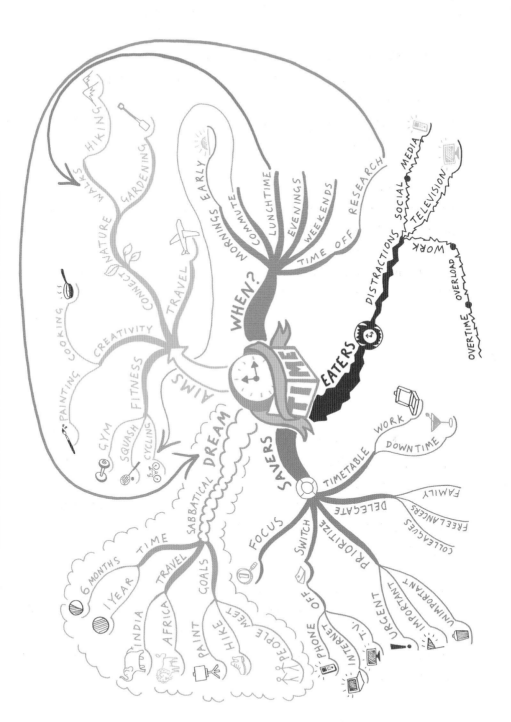

As a Mind Map like this is all about freeing yourself up to express your creativity, try to be as inventive as possible in your use of imagery. The example on page 109 is full of inspiring images, including a ribbon-wrapped clock representing the gift of time that you are giving yourself and illustrations expressing goals, such as doing more painting, hiking and travelling.

You can use a Mind Map not only to find out exactly what you want to do in your spare time but also to work out when you can do it: some activities you might be able to enjoy at lunchtimes or even during your commute, while others you can fit in on weekday evenings or at the weekend. Perhaps you have a dream that would mean taking a sabbatical, such as travelling to Africa or India? If you do, put it on your Mind Map! Only by recognizing our goals can we make them happen.

Creativity can of course take many forms – from painting the ceiling of the Sistine Chapel to preparing a delicious lunch, from writing a book to throwing a party, from composing a symphony to playing the penny whistle. Whatever form creativity takes, a Mind Map can facilitate its expression.

A Creativity Workout

In Chapter 1 (see page 33), I explained the concept of Radiant Thinking and introduced you to the Human Language. We discovered how every human – you and me included – is fluent in the twin faculties of association and imagination from birth. Now I'd like to invite you to play a little game.

I have used versions of this exercise for many years when teaching Mind Mapping and memory-improvement techniques, and I was intrigued to discover the late great British poet Ted Hughes simultaneously developed a similar practice when showing his students how to write poetry. It's an exercise that reveals the creative spark that exists within each and every one of us. Have a dictionary to hand before you start.

- **Pick an object at random. This could be something that you see in the room or something that pops into your mind.**

- **Close your eyes, flick open the dictionary and place your finger on the page.**

- **Now, open your eyes and write down the word you have chosen.**

- **Repeat nine times, randomly dipping into the dictionary, until you have ten different words.**

- **Now find as many associations as you can between the object and each of those words.**

If you find this a little difficult to do at first, keep going and I promise you will find associations – however outlandish these seem!

After approximately 20 minutes, read through your connections.

Pretty creative, aren't you?

How to Live Creatively

Phil Chambers is a World Mind Mapping Champion, the Chief Arbiter of the World Memory Sports Council, a successful businessman and the author of *How to Train Your Memory*. He explains how Mind Maps have informed his creative thinking for three decades:

> Mind Maps helped me revise for exams at school. At the time they were little more than spider diagrams with lots of colour but lacking structure and including phrases. However, they were still significantly more useful than lists. At university my style improved and I had big Mind Maps adorning my bedroom walls.
>
> I now use Mind Maps to structure my writing. It makes sense to think clearly about what you want to say before sitting down to type. By separating the process of thinking from writing, I have very little redrafting to do and end up with a more coherent document. This is especially important when writing books.
>
> As an instructor, a large part of my job is creating presentations. To prepare, I make a Mind Map with the different topics, actions and flow of concepts. This allows me to construct appropriate slides and I can then use the Mind Map as the perfect illustration to guide students through the session.

A major problem with a busy life is planning your use of time. A Mind Map is the perfect tool for this, from a quick daily plan to a broader monthly one. I like to have a Mind Map next to my desk and a highlighter so I can strike out tasks once completed.

As Mind Maps can be works of art, I like to give them as gifts in the form of birthday and Christmas cards. It has become a tradition for me each year to take a Christmas song and create an animated Mind Map of the lyrics involving humour and images. As you can see from the Mind Map *below*, Mind Mapping plays a pivotal role in much of my life.

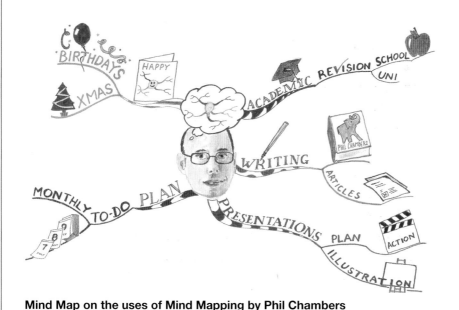

Mind Map on the uses of Mind Mapping by Phil Chambers

KEY MIND MAP APPLICATION 5: WELLBEING

There is a proven positive relationship between physical wellbeing and mental performance. Today, lobby groups are campaigning to make the government acknowledge the connection between the two when making policy, as they argue mental health and physical health should not be thought of as separate entities.

I have always enjoyed physical activities such as rowing and running; and I am a firm believer that, in order to flourish mentally, you should care for your physical wellbeing. I also believe the opposite holds true: that poor mental health can be detrimental to physical health and even make some conditions worse.

Five-time Olympic gold medallist Sir Steve Redgrave has a well-developed understanding of the mind–body connection. He has stressed how vital the brain is to any sporting achievement, and has said, "When you compete at a high level, you have to be very strong mentally.". He is also a firm supporter of the work that me and my fellow Mind Mappers do, saying:

> **"Tony Buzan is one of the very few people I have met who really understands so completely how important the brain is to any sportsman or woman."**

Achieve Holistic Wellbeing

These days we understand that getting in great shape is not about focusing solely on exercise and restrictive diets, but about promoting all-round wellbeing, including nourishing our bodies properly, getting enough sleep, destressing and doing the things that make us happy. The good news is

MIND MAP FOR ACHIEVING HOLISTIC WELLBEING

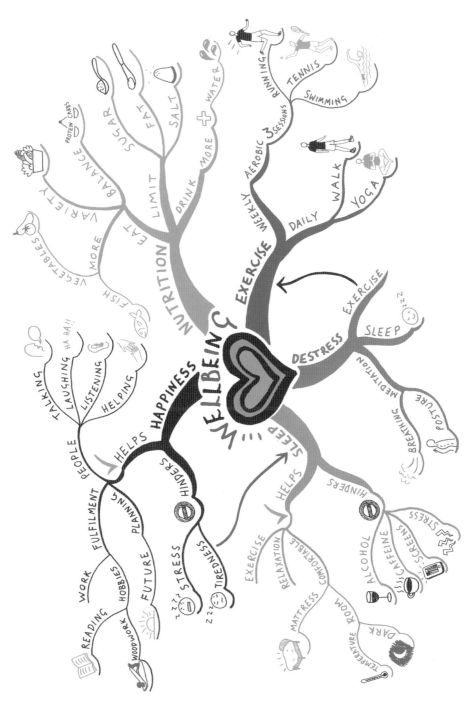

that you don't have to spend a fortune on the services of a personal trainer or a lifestyle coach to help you feel and look great. Instead, use a Mind Map to create a personal holistic wellbeing plan of your own. Try to create images that will inspire you by radiating vitality and good health. Your main branches could reflect the key areas that contribute to your all-round wellbeing – the example on page 115 explores nutrition, exercise, destressing, sleep and happiness, but you might choose to focus on slightly different areas. As you fill in the sub-branches, looking at what supports your overall wellbeing and what hinders it, you will see how certain activities benefit you in many different ways. Perhaps exercise crops up not only as a wellbeing target of its own but also as a means of getting more sleep and destressing, which in turn helps promote happiness. In my experience, mental health and physical fitness are inextricable.

The more you work on your Mind Map, the more it will speak to you and offer you all the coaching you need!

Make a Mind Map your Number One personal trainer!

Eat Well

A more targeted Mind Map can also be used for nutrition, to make sure that you eat a healthy diet that includes a balance of all the major food groups (carbohydrates, proteins, dairy, fruit and vegetables, and fats and sugars).

You can use a Mind Map as a weekly meal planner by adapting your personal weekly planner Mind Map (see page 83) to focus on food rather than activities. The sub-branches could list the day's main meals, spreading out to detail the ingredients of each meal, along with its nutritional value. If you create an Mind Map focusing on eating well at the start of each week, you'll provide yourself with a handy shopping list.

If you are looking to include more vitamins and minerals in your diet, try focusing on your diet even more closely and create a Mind Map that lists them, along with the foods in which they are found. It's not always obvious where the main vitamins are found, so I've provided a list below.

Once you have decided on your central image (perhaps a bottle with the label "V & M" or, if you like drawing people, a picture of someone who's just radiating health), create branches for each of the main vitamin groups and minerals, then fill the sub-branches with wonderful symbols and images, perhaps using chunking to group them together. Use connecting arrows to underscore links between different groups. Then you can frame your magnificently illustrated Mind Map and hang it on the wall as a guide and inspiration to ensure you always eat a balanced and varied diet.

Vitamin/Mineral	Sources include
Vitamin A	cheese, eggs, oily fish, milk and yoghurt, liver and liver paté
B vitamins	peas, fruit, eggs, meat, vegetables
Folic acid:	broccoli, spinach, asparagus, peas, chickpeas
Vitamin C	citrus fruits, green and red peppers, strawberries, potatoes
Vitamin D	oily fish, red meat, liver, egg yolk
Vitamin E	seeds and nuts, olive oil, wheatgerm
Vitamin K	leafy green vegetables, vegetable oils, cereal grains
Calcium	milk, leafy green vegetables, tofu, soya, nuts
Iodine	fish, shellfish
Iron	meat, beans, nuts, dark-green leafy vegetables

KEY MIND MAP APPLICATION 6: MEMORY

As I've explained, I originally invented the Mind Map as a mnemonic tool, and it remains one of the most powerful means available for remembering vast quantities of information. Every use of Mind Maps covered in this chapter strengthens your memory in some way, from embedding the key points of a text in your brain in order to revise for an exam or write an essay, to remembering all the things you need to achieve over the coming week and reminding yourself to exercise and eat well.

We have seen how important the power of association is in the formation of a Mind Map: when combined with imagination, it feeds and waters the branches of the Mind Map, encouraging them to radiate organically from the central image. In addition to this, association acts as a key to memory itself.

In 1969, American cognitive scientists Allan M. Collins and M. Ross Quillian tested the way in which memories are organized for efficient enquiry, allowing us to dip into our memory banks without a moment's hesitation. They found that our semantic memory (a way in which we make sense of the world through logic and language) is organized like a library of sorts, with interrelated categories or nodes representing specific features or concepts, which are then connected to one another.

Our individual experiences shape these connections, which means that everybody has their own spider's web of associations: for example, "bird" is connected to "flight" is connected to "sky". A Mind Map works in harmony with this process by taking a subject and then using imagination and association to link together everything the Mind Mapper knows about it.

The individual nature of our semantic networks is one reason why a Mind Map is inevitably such a personal creation: to get the most out of one and

Spouting Nonsense by Heart

Edward Lear (1812–88) was an English artist and author who, among his other notable accomplishments, was Queen Victoria's art teacher and the author of some wonderful nonsense verse. He is probably best remembered today for "The Owl and the Pussycat".

We will be leaving those feathered and furry friends to their own devices today. Instead, I invite you to read the following limerick by Lear:

> **There was an Old Man who said, "Hush!**
> **I perceive a young bird in this bush!"**
> **When they said, "Is it small?"**
> **He replied,"Not at all!**
> **It is four times as big as the bush!"**

Now make a Mind Map of the limerick that includes its imagery.

When you have finished, study your Mind Map for about five to ten minutes, or until you think you've memorized the information on it. Set it to one side.

On a fresh sheet of paper, recall and write out the limerick from memory. How did you do?

If you enjoy the process, make a Mind Map for a longer poem. Before you know it, you will be able to commit whole ballads to memory!

to improve your chances of memorizing the information in it, you will have to create your own Mind Map rather than rely on one that has been made by somebody else. This is one reason why I personally prefer hand-drawn Mind Maps to digital versions, useful though those can be. It can also be slightly more difficult to understand someone else's Mind Map, as the way that person associates and links information may not be the same as yours, and that slight difficulty will make the Mind Map less useful to you.

When we are attempting to revise and memorize information, problems tend to occur in the short-term memory, as this is where new information is initially collected before being passed on to the long-term memory. Earlier in this chapter (see page 72), we learned how the psychologist George Armitage Miller discovered that the short-term memory can only hold approximately seven pieces of information. If this information is to be retained by the long-term memory, it has to be rehearsed before it can be passed on, which is why last-minute cramming for an exam can be so difficult: for information to be efficiently remembered, it has to be collated and connected in some way. And this, of course, is where chunking in Mind Maps can come into its own as a means of recalling data (see page 72).

The very act of physically creating a Mind Map helps to make the information in it more memorable, enabling you to visualize and recall the process of creating it. Through the use of colour and images, a Mind Map engages the brain and imprints itself on the memory.

If you wish to recall the information in your Mind Map precisely, I would suggest that you take your time to study it carefully and revise its connections, images and branches. The more you do this, the more decisively the information will be imprinted on your memory.

From planning a party to salvaging a relationship, memorizing lyrics or making a polished, professional presentation, a Mind Map makes matters manageable by breaking down a task, text or situation into its elements. It highlights connections and invites the brain to engage as an active participant in the process by looking for solutions, committing details to memory and working on outcomes, rather than remaining a passive receptacle for information.

However, there are many times when something that appears to be a Mind Map is *not* in fact a Mind Map. How can you tell a true Mind Map from a false one? The answer to that question can be found in the next chapter.

3

What Is *Not* a Mind Map?

This chapter dispels some of the myths that have sprung up around the Mind Map, and examines cases of mistaken identity, explaining why fake Mind Maps are not nearly as helpful as those that follow the Laws of Mind Mapping. It provides handy tips for creating genuine Mind Maps as well as guidance on how to spot the imposters!

Myths and Misconceptions

Since their invention in the 1950s and 1960s, Mind Maps have gone on to help people all around the world – and they continue to transform lives today. It's the greatest reward I could have ever hoped for; I never cease to be delighted by the global reach and appeal of Mind Mapping. By working with our innate Human Language, harnessing the twin forces of imagination and association, the Mind Map has become a thinking tool that transcends cultural divisions.

Given the popularity of Mind Maps, perhaps it isn't surprising, then, that over the decades various myths and misconceptions have arisen around them. My heart sinks whenever I come across some of the more common misunderstandings, such as the mistaken belief that Mind Maps and spider diagrams are the same thing.

Moreover, there is a real risk that any confusion between Mind Maps and diagrams such as concept maps and pyramid diagrams could compromise the integrity of the Mind Map itself, as it means some people may not appreciate the power of Mind Mapping or realize Mind Maps' *full* potential. Likewise, I find it frustrating whenever I meet individuals who have been exposed to poor training by those who purport to be experts in Mind Mapping, despite being poorly trained themselves.

Let's sort the wheat from the chaff, and clear up any confusion about what a Mind Map is and what it is not.

Myth Busting

In Chapters 1 and 2, we looked briefly at the history of Mind Maps in relation to the development of visual thought, and the way in which the deep ancestry of this thinking tool can be found in the stunning cave art of our

Stone Age forebears. We touched on the pioneering practices of cultures such as ancient Greece, and considered the work of geniuses such as Charles Darwin, who used diagrams to develop their ideas.

Unfortunately, there are some today who confuse similarity with sameness, and who therefore credit the Phoenician philosopher Porphyry of Tyros (*c.*232–303 CE) with the origins of the Mind Map. A Neoplatonist, Porphyry organized the ideas of Aristotle on a diagram traditionally described as an *arbor*, or tree, the layout of which is not dissimilar to the Kabbalistic Tree of Life in the Jewish mystical tradition. There is no central image in Porphyry's diagram (see Chapter 1, page 45), nor are there any illustrations; the words are placed in an ordered manner in spheres and along connecting pathways. The thinking here is not radiant, as it is in a Mind Map.

Similarly, I sometimes come across people who suggest that Leonardo da Vinci invented Mind Mapping. Perhaps this isn't surprising: after all, this pioneering thinker was so ahead of his time that he was sketching incredible contraptions such as wing devices and the human-powered "ornithopter" 400 years before the Wright brothers successfully flew the first powered aeroplane in 1903. Da Vinci's combination of words and images in his notes certainly helped shape the early stages of my research into the nature of human thought; yet this great artist and thinker did not use colour schematically in his diagrams, which, as we have seen, is a key element in Mind Mapping.

Likewise, there are those who credit the invention of the Mind Map to Sir Isaac Newton (1642–1727), the English scientist who discovered gravity after observing an apple falling from an apple tree. This distinguished scientist used intriguing concept diagrams to chart his ideas, but these too were monochromatic and took the form of a "tree" growing upward rather than expanding radiantly, like a starburst, the way in which a Mind Map spreads across the page. While the thinking of geniuses such as da Vinci and Newton is clearly timeless, to confuse centuries-old diagrams with modern Mind Maps is a little like mistaking a penny farthing bicycle for a supercharged motorcycle!

A Case of Mistaken Identity

People who are new to Mind Maps and who have yet to master the Laws of Mind Mapping (see Chapter 2, page 60) may at first find themselves creating diagrams that superficially resemble Mind Maps, but that turn out to be something completely different, such as a spider diagram, pyramid diagram, concept map, fishbone diagram or sunburst chart.

SPIDER DIAGRAMS

Like Mind Maps, spider diagrams (see box, *opposite*) can be used for planning essays and for organizing ideas. They often have a highly structured layout, with legs projecting from a central idea. However, unlike Mind Maps, they don't always use colour and very rarely use images. A spider diagram's legs are usually linear and spindly, rather than organic and varying in thickness.

PYRAMID DIAGRAMS

Pyramid diagrams are similar to spider diagrams but they place a greater emphasis on hierarchy. While the main idea sits in the centre of a spider diagram or a Mind Map, in a pyramid diagram the core concept is positioned at the top with the associated ideas progressing down from it in an ordered manner. This means the tendency is for the eye to scan the page from top to bottom in a one-directional, rigid, linear manner, rather than ranging

Pyramid diagram

Give the Spider Its Legs Back

Take a look at the spider diagram below:

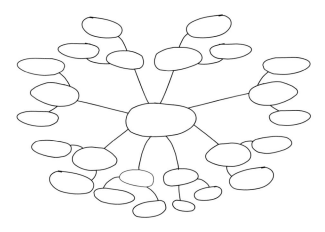

Now turn back to "How to Create a Mind Map" in Chapter 1 (page 27), and read through the seven steps again.

When you are ready, have a go at making a spider diagram using the template above as a rough guide, then use this information to create a Mind Map.

Once you are finished, compare the two.

Which image is the most striking, appealing and memorable?

Why? Take a look back at the Laws of Mind Mapping in Chapter 2 (page 60). In what ways do the Laws make a Mind Map more visually appealing than a spider diagram?

freely over the diagram in a way that encourages the brain to come up with fresh connections and new insights.

CONCEPT MAPS

Concept maps present ideas and information in the form of words and phrases that are placed in boxes or circles. Like pyramid diagrams, these units are connected in a downward-branching hierarchical structure, meaning that concept maps tend to be read from the top down, with all the restrictions that that entails. Their connecting arrows are usually labelled, as are the branches in Mind Maps. However, the label on a connecting

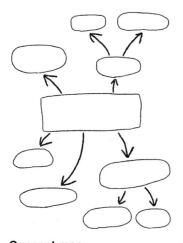

arrow in a concept map can take the form of a phrase rather than a single word, so loses the impact that a single keyword has. Moreover, colours and images are not a feature of these graphical tools, lessening the visual impact of a concept map, as well as its appeal to the brain. Concept maps often have a pedagogical function, presenting information that is to be learned by rote, whereas Mind Maps can be used as a technique for brainstorming and devising new strategies, as well as in many other creative ways.

Concept map

FISHBONE DIAGRAMS

Also known as Ishikawa diagrams after they were popularized in the 1960s by the Japanese organizational theorist Kaoru Ishikawa (1915–89), fishbone diagrams take their name from their shape. The "bones" of the diagram relate to particular factors or considerations, while the cumulative effect

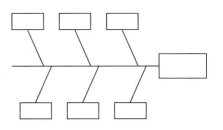

Fishbone diagram

sits at the "head", meaning that fishbone diagrams are usually read from left to right (or right to left if you are in Japan!). They are linear, monochrome and the focus in them is on cause and effect rather than on igniting the powers of the imagination and association in order to stimulate the brain.

SUNBURST CHART

Also known as a sunburst diagram, ring chart, multilevel pie chart, belt chart or a radial tree map, a sunburst chart is compact and formed of concentric circles which represent layers of hierarchical data. Each layer is divided into categories or segments, which are often depicted in different colours. The charts do not use imagery. While perhaps useful for summarizing data, they can be hard to read and are not a great tool for inspired creative thinking.

Sunburst chart

How to Spot a Non-Mind Map

You now know what a Mind Map is, and what it is not! When the Laws of Mind Mapping are neglected, the result is all too often monotony, a lack of order and clarity, and sprawling confusion. Or you may come across a diagram that superficially resembles a Mind Map, but is actually something else altogether.

Generally speaking, Mind Maps are much more adept at releasing the power of creative thinking than other types of visual tool. While there are key steps and essential elements in a Mind Map, the imagery in each one is unique to that Mind Map: there is no formal iconography, nor a rigorous sense in which a Mind Map can be "right or wrong" in the way that a graphic such as a pie chart could be mathematically flawed, for example.

Mind Maps do not generally relate to steps, systems or processes, yet they are full of movement and are steeped in an innate logic. They have been called illogical by some because they are not based on lists, lines and numbers – yet nothing could be further from the truth. A Mind Map, on one level, is a superbly logical thinking tool, because in a Mind Map things only connect to other elements through the power of association, meaning there is a natural, causal link between them. After all, logic is the ability to make appropriate associations in order to come to a rational conclusion.

Moreover, in addition to representing information, the very act of creating a Mind Map stimulates the brain and engages the memory. It is a manifestation of the thoughts and ideas of its individual creator.

A Mind Map's use of colour, imagery and visual connections is informal, organic – and essential to its proper functioning.

A Mind Map can become a thing of considerable beauty in its own right. I have seen some Mind Maps that have literally taken my breath away, such as the fine example from China on page 132. This Mind Map was created by Richard Lin, a former businessman who is today a successful life coach, public speaker, university mentor and master Mind Mapper.

Take a long, hard look at this wonderful Mind Map. What imagery can you see? What do you think this Mind Map is about?

Did you notice the computer screen underneath the central heading? Richard's Mind Map is describing the brain as a "neck-top computer",

To check whether you are looking at a true Mind Map, consider the following:

Is there a clear central concept?

Is there a clear central image depicting that concept?

Does the diagram radiate from the centre?

Is there always one word per branch?

Are there any images?

Is colour used throughout?

Is the Mind Map clear?

Is the Mind Map natural and organic in appearance?

Is the Mind Map highly visually appealing?

If the answer to any of these questions is "no", you are not looking at a true Mind Map.

Mind Map on the brain as a neck-top computer by Richard Lin

and each of the branches relates to a key principle of Mind Mapping, such as the use of colour, dimension and association. It's a masterpiece of Mind Mapping and I love it!

With time and practice, you too will develop your own unique style when Mind Mapping.

And that's really something to be celebrated!

Imagine Losing the Laws

Take a look at one of the Mind Maps you created while reading through Chapter 2.

- **Imagine your Mind Map with no central image, the brain and heart of it extracted.**

- **Imagine your Mind Map with no colour, and consider its lack of power.**

- **Imagine your Mind Map with only straight lines, and think of its rigidity and its lack of appeal.**

- **Imagine your Mind Map with no images throughout, its life blood diluted.**

- **Imagine your Mind Map with more than one word per branch, and visualize how clumsy it would be.**

- **Imagine your Mind Map branches and keywords are of unequal length: see how its structure collapses.**

- **Now imagine the accumulating disadvantages of eliminating all of the Laws – and picture what a lawless, chaotic and disintegrating state that would be …**

4

Solution Finding

At some stage in your Mind Mapping
journey, you may feel that Mind Maps
just aren't working for you. Please
don't give up! This chapter offers all the
solutions you need, including tips on
asking the right questions, dealing with
a cluttered or messy page, and why you
should let repetition in a Mind Map be
your guide. It will show you that Mind
Maps can always help you find the right
path – all you need to do is persevere.

Perseverance is the Key to Success

In their use of the powers of association and imagination, and their inherent logic, the Laws of Mind Mapping are a manifestation of the more general laws of good thinking. Just like the branches of a Mind Map spread into new areas, the Laws of Mind Mapping can be applied in an infinite variety of ways. They are always there as a map to guide you, and as a safety net ready to catch you, so turn to them, should you ever find yourself in need of encouragement or reassurance.

Don't be discouraged when you run into obstacles with your Mind Mapping. Remember that you have already reached a significant stage in your Mind Mapping journey. The fact that you are running into difficulties could simply be an indication that you are taking your Mind Mapping practice to a new level. If you persevere in facing up to each apparent obstacle as it arises, and complete all the exercises in this book, by the time you finish reading it, you will be well on the way to Mind Mapping mastery.

If you are encountering problems, perhaps come to a point in your journey where you need to clarify both your approach to Mind Mapping and your thinking. You could, for example, find it helpful to reread Chapter 3, "What Is *Not* a Mind Map". I have found that many people who say they are experiencing difficulties in Mind Mapping are not in fact working with Mind Maps at all, but are making spider diagrams. Sometimes, they have forgotten the importance of colour or of using keywords.

Often, it is not the Mind Map causing the problem, but a person's fears around it. Fear is the great mind killer. If you were ever to find yourself on a boat in turbulent seas, you would hold tight to the ropes, steer the rudder and take control of the helm; in the same way, if you ever find yourself in rocky waters when Mind Mapping, tighten your command of the Laws.

Check – and check again – that each Mind Map is following the Laws of Mind Mapping.

Take a good look at a Mind Map that doesn't seem to be working for you. Now turn back to the Laws of Mind Mapping in Chapter 2 (see page 60), and read them through again carefully.

Imagine your Mind Map is a Formula 1 racing car: during the course of a race, you steer into the pit stop so that mechanics can check and service your car, and send you safely on your way. In the same way, make an effort to service your Mind Map and to keep on making sure that it is being served by the Laws.

If you have a Mind Map that strikes you as being potentially troublesome, keep a copy of the Laws in front of you and refer back to it while you examine the Mind Map in more detail:

- **Are you working on a piece of unlined paper that is at least A4 in size and placed horizontally?**
- **Is the central image positioned in the middle of the page and drawn in at least three colours?**
- **Is the central image eye-catching?**
- **If the central image includes a word, is that word in 3D or made to look interesting typographically?**
- **Are the main branches in different colours?**
- **Is there only one word per branch?**
- **Have the branches sprouted healthy numbers of sub-branches?**
- **Have you used images throughout?**

If the answer to any of these questions is no, make another version of your Mind Map that sticks tightly to the Laws. In all probability, you will achieve a much better result.

**A Mind Map always works
when it is worked well.**

Ask the Right Question

Good questions make all the difference when it comes to achieving excellent results. Asking the right question is like aiming an arrow at the bull's eye of your goal, and drawing an arrow from the quiver of your curiosity and intellect.

Whenever you create a Mind Map, think carefully about the question or topic that you wish to address. An effective question or topic will:

- **Trigger the powers of association and imagination**
- **Be open, allowing consideration and assessment rather than closed yes/no responses**
- **Inspire critical and analytic thinking**
- **Create clarity**
- **Challenge assumptions**
- **Stimulate breakthrough thinking**
- **Achieve a balance between the content (who? what? when?) and the process (how? why?)**
- **Inspire a positive reaction**

Poorly formulated questions lead to flawed answers. To avoid ambiguity in your answers, keep your central question short, clear and precise. When you begin to consider a topic in a Mind Map, focus on it like a movie director with a zoom lens.

Mind Map a Good Question

Read through the bullet points *opposite* again. Keeping these points foremost in your thoughts, make a Mind Map that captures them and considers the nature of an effective question or topic.

Remember that an artist's greatest fear often takes the form of a blank canvas. The most important step is simply to make those first marks. Use this Mind Map to help you eliminate the fear of committing yourself to paper. Make your first marks, and then keep on making them! Remember: Mind Mapping is an ongoing process, in which you are invited to ask question after question.

Look at your Mind Map. Ask yourself about your central question. As you continue Mind Mapping, always double-check that it works and be ready to readjust if necessary.

Use Simple yet Powerful Images

Like the question or topic you wish to consider, keep your central image simple yet striking – so that it packs the punch of a brand's logo, yet with a dash more colour. Keep the lines clean and clear, and make your central image focused.

The spread of your Mind Map across the page, as its branches become increasingly filled with symbols and words, is a wonderful testimony to the fact that your brain is generating more ideas. Should your Mind Map appear overcrowded, you have simply reached the stage of generating mini Mind Maps – or "child" Mind Maps, which often have the potential to grow into big adult Mind Maps themselves (see page 142).

Make Space for Your Ideas

Let's say the problem doesn't seem to lie in your central image. You like the central image: it's colourful, eye-catching and effective. It immediately triggers all sorts of associations in your imagination.

If this is the case, take a look at the main branches of your Mind Map. Are you looking at fertile woodland or an unruly tangle of brambles? Can you still "see the wood for the trees"?

Clarity is an important element in a Mind Map. Rather like the focus on asymmetry and space in *ikebana*, the Japanese art of flower arranging, the area around each branch in your Mind Map is as significant in some respects as the branch itself.

"Negative" space in artistic creations helps to define the boundaries of the object and adds balance to a composition.

Embrace Messiness

A "messy" Mind Map, however, is far from being a disaster. There is no need to give yourself a hard time if you end up with one. Usually, a messy Mind Map is simply a reflection of your thought processes at the time you created it. Perhaps you were quickly Mind Mapping to record a phone conversation or take notes for a lecture? If so, your Mind Map will reflect the challenges of Mind Mapping at speed while following the twists and turns of a discussion or talk.

If you believe your Mind Map is messy, I would ask you to adjust your camera lens and take another look: even if your Mind Map spreads chaotically all over the page and is hard to read, please be happy with what

A Note on Messiness

It's time to rethink our definition of the word "messy"!

Traditionally, notions of "tidy" and "messy" note-taking have been defined – dare I say it – arbitrarily by those in the academic arena who are used to linear ways of thinking. For them, "neat" notes stick to the lines on a page like small birds glued by lime to twigs, whereas "messy" notes take flight and hop about, combining words, signs, symbols and numbers.

There are even those who would describe the notes of geniuses such as Leonardo da Vinci and Charles Darwin as being "messy". The fact is that we should be rethinking our definitions:

Colourful, branching, "messy" notes are anything but messy in terms of their power and impact!

Given that linear notes make association very difficult, lose profound connections and eliminate the Human Language from the brain, should we really be calling them "neat"? I would argue that linear notes are actually truly messy in many respects in that they mess up thinking, logic, creativity, confidence, enjoyment and the potential for fun. Indeed, I would go so far as to say they mess up life itself!

you've achieved! While your Mind Map may not be a work of great beauty, it will nevertheless be a valuable first draft that can be used as the basis for a second Mind Map. After all, most of the great artists made sketches before finishing their masterpieces.

Before you begin work on a second Mind Map, double-check whether the organization of your first draft is flawed. Are some of the associations weak or were they made in error?

Remember how, in Chapter 2 (see page 104), Marek Kasperski likened a Mind Map to a garden? In your second Mind Map, prune away any unnecessary branches and sub-branches to give yourself clarity. If necessary, reorganize the main branches so that the sequence of your Basic Ordering Ideas (BOIs) is underpinned by logic and numerical order. For those branches that you wish to keep, make sure they are firmly fixed in place and spread pleasingly – like a fruit tree supported by a sturdy trellis.

Once you have cut away any redundant or repeated information on your branches, new shoots are likely to appear that will produce fruit in the form of original ideas and associations.

Begin your Mind Map again.
How are you going to improve it?

Sow Mini Mind Maps

In the process of revisiting your Mind Map, you may find that some ideas or issues have been exposed that could be usefully turned into mini Mind Maps, especially if developing them on the master Mind Map will make it problematically complex and difficult to decipher. Mini Mind Maps orbit the main Mind Map like moons around a planet. They explore aspects of the main Mind Map in closer detail without cluttering it up.

Provided there is enough room, a mini Mind Map or two can sit on the same page as the master Mind Map. If there isn't space, give them a page of their own. Think of a family in which, over time, a child has grown to the point of needing a room of their own. Treat these mini Mind Maps as you would a real child: not with disdain, but with encouragement. Rather than respond to them with negativity, nurture them.

Mini Mind Maps are especially rewarding tools if you find your master Mind Map raises more questions than answers. Use a mini Mind Map to address any new questions as well as tackle offshoots and digressions. You can even use mini Mind Maps to explore two sides of an argument, which is especially useful when writing an essay, for instance. (See also Chapter 5, page 169 for using Mind Maps in conflict resolution.)

Let Repetition Guide You

Every now and again, you will find that a seemingly unimportant word appears repeatedly in a Mind Map, on one branch, then another and another. This is not a problem. This is a breakthrough.

Through repetition, a keyword becomes a

key key word

or even a

key key key word

A word that emigrates to another branch of a Mind Map is not unnecessary or boring, but the exact opposite: it reinforces the strength of the idea that it embodies.

If you notice a word is repeated, underline it to make it stand out. If it appears three times, put a small box around it wherever it appears: it is clearly important. If it appears four times or more, it is shouting out for your attention! Draw the boxes around it in three dimensions. Now link the boxes to form a giant box around your whole Mind Map. Put this giant box in three dimensions as well.

Your Mind Map is now held within a larger framework, as a word that you originally thought relatively insignificant turns out to be of primary importance.

This represents a paradigm shift in your thinking – and is therefore a major leap forward in the way you are tackling an issue – because it shows that you are reframing your understanding and approach to a subject.

I strongly recommend that you use the word that has made itself known to you in this way as the new central image in your next Mind Map on this subject.

Deal with Indecision

Often the actual process of creating a Mind Map leads to a clear solution by providing a balanced overview of a situation. If your Mind Map doesn't invite you to choose a clear path of action, it is time to engage the powers of your intuition. Toss a coin and decide – heads or tails – which of the options you are going to pursue. Take note of the strength of your reaction and whether it is one of disappointment or joy; then allow your feelings to decide which choice is the right one for you.

If you still can't decide, dig deeper into your dilemma through the use of further Mind Maps and mini Mind Maps: do not procrastinate. Procrastination is mentally draining and counterproductive, whereas pursuing a clear course of action is liberating, energizing and leads to direct lived experience, even if that experience may not always fulfil expectations.

It is always better to be proactive and to do something than to wallow unproductively in the pit of inertia.

Keep Going!

If you produce a Mind Map and find that you have a strong negative reaction to it, do not be dismayed!

> **Persistence is key in Mind Mapping, and I would urge you to "try, try and TRY again"!**

This is the mantra of every teacher; persistence is all if you wish to achieve mastery in any field – including Mind Mapping. Mind Maps will strengthen your ability to persist as they continue to offer up solutions for you, help you to dissolve problems and, in the process, give you the energy to keep on trying.

I have mentioned before how you do not need to possess great artistic skill to become an accomplished Mind Mapper: the more Mind Maps you create, the better you will inevitably become at them. However, if you really feel inhibited about your drawing skills, you could find iMindMap software useful, especially if you draw on this in conjunction with creating Mind Maps by hand. This software automatically generates thick, organic branches for your BOIs, and smaller branches for sub-branches. It also includes a library containing thousands of high-quality images. (See Chapter 6, page 198, for more information.)

If you ever encounter a obstacle when you are Mind Mapping, remember that this is not designed to be a linear process. You do not need to keep banging your head against a problem. Simply sidestep it elegantly and explore another route!

Get Back on the Horse That Bucked You

Perhaps the very idea of creating a Mind Map has begun to seem like a daunting prospect: you are anxious about not getting it "right"; you think you don't have enough good ideas; you don't like the way you draw; you are disappointed by the end results. Here's what I would suggest:

Mind Map your worries away!

Mind Maps can be an excellent resource for self-analysis and for tackling personal problems such as anxiety, shyness, excessive perfectionism, feeling down, and disappointment. If you find that you aren't happy with your Mind Mapping results, make a Mind Map about your experience.

You could, for example, start with a central image showing yourself looking downhearted. Now do a quick-fire Mind Map, expressing openly and honestly whatever mixed thoughts and feelings you have had about the Mind Mapping process.

Your next step is to work up this draft into a more balanced and analytical Mind Map, with Basic Ordering Ideas (BOIs) that explore your emotions in more depth. Consider, for example:

- **The actual nature of your feelings – whether there are any layers to them**
- **The physical sensation of them**
- **How they influence your behaviour**
- **How they impact on your life**

- **Other situations in which you find you experience similar feelings**
- **Past events in which these feelings could have their origins**
- **Any outside help you need in order to tackle these feelings**

Examine each aspect of your emotions and the experiences that cause or relate to them. Once you have done this and have a clearer understanding of what is happening to you, you will find you are well on your way to exorcizing any emotional bugbears that are souring your enjoyment of Mind Mapping. Often the simple act of writing down a problem can diffuse it and help get it into perspective.

Solve Any Problem with Mind Mapping

Have you ever lain awake in the middle of the night, unable to sleep, tortured by a problem? The longer you lie there worrying about it, the worse your problem seems to become. Every time you think about it, another complication comes to the fore until the whole conundrum seems like an elaborate Celtic knot with no beginning or end.

When you rise the next morning, the problem can often take on different proportions in the clear light of day. Perhaps it no longer seems so daunting or impossible to solve. Often a moment of calm reflection is all that is needed. Indeed, maybe all you need to do is write it down to get to grips with it … To create a moment of calm and get this problem in perspective, make a Mind Map of it.

Start by drawing a central image that either relates to the issue specifically or more generally deals with the idea of "problem-solving". Through your branches you might want to start by defining the problem and its causes, and then go to explore the effects, negative and positive. One branch could deal with how to find help in handling the problem; remember that your own response to a difficult situation is the only one that you can fully control and self-help can be just as important as assistance from others. Then your Mind Map can move on to the planning and, finally, the acting stages of solving a problem.

Be sure to keep the words and images on your Mind Map positive and inspiring, so that your thinking is Radiant rather than reductive. Avoid using too many negative words, as these can be diminishing and unproductive. The images can act as a real inspiration as well as a reminder of what you need to do – in the example *opposite*, a memorable glowing heart symbolizes "bravery" while an open door stands for "openness". Keep your symbols in mind and, using the overview provided by a Mind Map, you will begin to see your way toward a workable solution.

As a Mind Map mimics the brain's own way of working and stimulates it into action, the act of making this Mind Map will engage your thinking processes: instead of remaining frozen with anxiety or falling into flight mode, the process of Mind Mapping will give you the energy and clarity to fight and resolve your dilemma. By analysing your feelings in this way, you may well find that you have now identified and can tackle emotional tendencies that have been detracting from your enjoyment of life generally.

Rather than closing down with linear notes, let a Mind Map open you up to the world!

PROBLEM SOLVING

PROBLEM

DEFINE
ISSUE — SINGLE? MULTIPLE?
WHOSE — YOURS? SOMEONE ELSE'S?
WHY? CAUSES — ROOT, CURRENT CONDITIONS

EFFECTS
NEGATIVE — PRACTICAL, FINANCIAL
FEELINGS — YOURS, OTHERS'
OPPORTUNITIES

HELP FROM OTHERS
ADVICE
PERSPECTIVE
SUPPORT

BE ONESELF
ACCEPT — CHANGE
FACE — CHALLENGE
BRAVE
OPEN

RELAX
EXERCISE
DOWNTIME
SLEEP — Zzz

PLAN
LISTEN
DISCUSS
THINK — BIG
CREATIVELY — MIND MAP, BRAINSTORM, DAYDREAM

ACT
KEEP GOING
EVALUATE — RETHINK
IMPLEMENT — SOLUTIONS
NEGOTIATE

The Magic of Thinking Big

Mind Maps are excellent path finders.

Arif Anis is a leading international coach and bestselling author who has the privilege of coaching top corporate leaders, heads of states, movie stars and CEOs; yet it wasn't always this way. He is living proof of Mind Maps' power to solve problems. Once downcast and confused, Mind Maps helped him solve the problem of where he was heading in life, and he has been using them ever since. Today he is a successful businessman and author, a powerhouse of ideas and an inspiration to all who meet him. Here is his story:

> As they say, if you are a lucky student and you want it enough, you don't find your teacher but your teacher finds you – so I met Mind Maps at a critical juncture in my life.
>
> I left university with a heavy heart after gaining a postgraduate in psychology. I was puzzled, confused and scared. Life outside the campus seemed really daunting. What to choose? Which way to go? What was my career going to be for the rest of my life? And what if I made a wrong choice? I was paralysed by fear of the unknown.
>
> Too many options were available to me and it was hard to separate them from each other. I seemed to have become lost in the abyss of life – and then I found Tony Buzan's bestselling Mind Mapping books in my local bookshop and life was never the same again.

I started drawing Mind Maps. Lousy ones in the beginning. But there was something in those colours and images … Slowly, the road started emerging and it became clearer with every passing step. At last I could see the highway – and where it was taking me. My confidence started seeping back. I was now a man with a mission who clearly knew what he wanted in his life and how to get there. I got the big picture with all of its sharpness and hues. It changed everything from then onward.

When I look back at my life and the major milestones, they have one thing in common: I find Mind Maps all around them. Be it my first job as a trainee psychologist; my preparation for the most competitive examination in Pakistan, which attracted the best of the best for coveted positions in the civilian bureaucracy; my wedding plans; or writing my bestselling books. Mind Maps brought synergy and clarity to my decisions and produced results.

Much to my own surprise, I was able to pass the toughest exam in the country after only 40 days' study. And I knew I could achieve much more in less time. My productivity quadrupled, as did my options and choices in life. I was not pushed or cajoled by life any more. I knew what I wanted and how to get there.

Today, I have the privilege of teaching Mind Maps to thousands of people in Pakistan. They include students, trainees, interns, officers, marketers, salespeople, doctors and many more. The practice has gone on to reach scores of colleges, universities, corporate organizations and training institutions, and inspired thousands of Mind Mappers to take on the world in their relevant disciplines.

Mind Maps also inspire my next generation. My sons Sarosh and Fariqlee were introduced to Mind Maps at the age of four and they instantly fell in love with the process. At first they used Mind Maps to express themselves and plan family vacations. Gradually they became hooked on them, and my wife Uzma and I would find Mind Maps everywhere – on the walls, in the closet and on the sofas. Today, they constitute one of the most essential tools in their study skills kit. More than this, Mind Mapping trained them to exercise their thinking muscles while tuning into their creative instincts.

I am proud to say we are a "Mind Mapper" family!

5

The Infinite Applications of Mind Maps

You have in your hands an incredibly powerful thinking tool, and now you are ready to take it to a higher level. What will you do with Mind Mapping next, and how will you use it to enhance your own life as well as the lives of others? This chapter suggests a huge range of different applications, and includes guidance on how to use advanced Mind Mapping techniques in the key areas of your life explored in Chapter 2: home, work, education, creativity, wellbeing and memory.

Tools for an Intuitive and Logical Approach

The Mind Map works with our innate Human Language. We saw in Chapter 2 how we are born fluent in this language (see page 34): even as babies we learn with a form of Mind Maps in our heads. As the Mind Map is based on the way we instinctively view the world, it naturally has infinite applications, each one as individual as we are.

Through its infinite applications, the Mind Map has evolved into a metalanguage: the language of language itself.

This metalanguage speaks to both the logical and intuitive sides of the brain. The emphasis in Mind Mapping on the twin forces of association and imagination means some people believe Mind Mapping must be unsuited to technical subjects or rational processes such as mathematics. This is simply untrue.

We have seen how Mind Maps are highly logical, in that they are rooted in the logic of association (see Chapter 3, page 130). They are extremely structured and subject to the Laws of Mind Mapping, which if followed will always ensure their clarity and usefulness. These Laws encourage people to take an ordered approach when structuring a Mind Map. Moreover, if they wish, those who are drawn toward logical ways of thinking can work through the associations one branch at a time before moving on to the next main branch in their Mind Maps.

The structure of Mind Maps makes them a good fit for subjects that lend themselves to categorization and to a consideration of processes, such as physics, chemistry and mathematics, as Dr Dilip Abayasekara described

Mind Maps as a Call to Action

Dominic O'Brien, who kindly supplied the Foreword for this book, has won World Memory Championships many times and is the bestselling author of books about memorization techniques. He is also a major advocate of the many benefits and applications of Mind Mapping:

> For me, Mind Maps are a great way of overcoming procrastination. Sometimes the thought of embarking on a new book or preparing a memory course can be daunting: with so many topics to cover, it's easy to fall in the "Where the heck do I start?" trap.
>
> By grabbing a blank A4 sheet of paper and placing it horizontally, I can dive straight into a project and chuck down my immediate ideas. More often than not, the first thoughts that fall out of my mind are the topics I most need to cover. Hence the Mind Map allows me to prioritize what is essential to the project.
>
> The fine-tuning of the precise order of topics is much easier if I literally have a picture of them, right there, in front of me. Typically I go through this first-step process when:

- **Writing a new book or article on memory**
- **Organizing a seminar or speaking engagement**
- **Preparing for an important meeting**
- **Assembling the background details of a new client**

- **Understanding a complex subject, whether politics or a scientific breakthrough**
- **Moving house or preparing a travel schedule**
- **Prioritizing the "to-dos"**

Probably the last one – 'prioritizing' – is the most beneficial and important use of a Mind Map for me. Sometimes it is too easy to get caught in the present and I can find myself honing in on the challenges of what turns out to be trivia. The to-do Mind Map allows me to step back and be reminded of the grand overview of what I want to achieve in life.

It's been said many times that Mind Mapping is the "Swiss army knife" for the brain. Well, in my experience that's the best description for it!

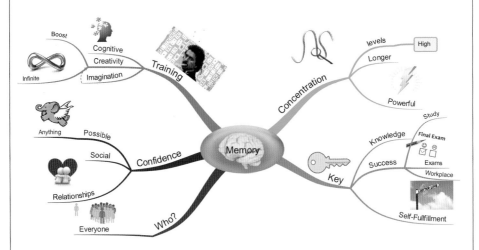

Mind Map on Mind Mapping's benefits for memory by Dominic O'Brien

in Chapter 2 (page 96), when discussing how he used Mind Maps in his lab work. They are useful tools for breaking down scientific topics into their component parts and providing an overview.

A Mind Map can also act as a direct stimulus, spurring us into activity. Here's a favourite quote of mine from the Scottish mountaineer and writer W.H. Murray, which pinpoints how everything seems to fall into place once we make a commitment to do something. And creating a Mind Map is the ideal way of making that commitment:

Concerning all acts of initiative (and creation), there is one elementary truth that ignorance of which kills countless ideas and splendid plans: that the moment one definitely commits oneself, then Providence moves too.

W. H. Murray, *The Scottish Himalaya Expedition*

The 99 Applications

Alongside the many stories I receive of people whose lives have been totally transformed by Mind Mapping, the evidence today of millions of Mind Maps and proto-Mind Maps on the Internet has made it increasingly obvious that the number of applications for a Mind Map is infinite!

Overleaf is a taster of a sample of these: 99 areas of enquiry that a Mind Map can help explore for the benefit of us all. Use this list as an inspiration and a starting point for your Mind Mapping adventures. I would be thrilled to hear how you get on.

TOP 99 MIND MAP APPLICATIONS

Home:

Arranging Travel	Family Connections	Planning for the Future
Charitable Activities	Flourishing Friendships	Relationships
Choosing a Baby's Name	Marital Harmony	Shopping
Choosing a Pet	Moving House	Throwing a Dinner Party
Diary Keeping	Packing for Journeys	Weighing Pros and Cons

Work:

Business Growth	Goal Setting	Organizing Ideas
Creating a CV	Making Decisions	Planning Meetings
Devising Strategies	Management	Presenting
Event Planning	Managing Business Contacts	Reaching Targets
Finding Employment	Managing Finances	Sales Strategies
Future Projections	Minuting Meetings	Summarizing Information
Getting Promoted	Organization	Team Analysis

Education:

Archaeology	Choosing a University	Explaining a Supernova
Astronomy	Coming Up with Definitions	Explaining a Tree's Structure
Biology	Economics	Geography
Botany	Engineering	Grammar
Chemistry	Explaining a Neuron	History

IT	Maths	Revision
Languages	Medicine	Sciences
Law	Physics	School Projects
Literature	Maths	Study Skills
Mapping the Cosmos	Politics	Zoology

Creativity:

Art	Decorating a Room	Music Appreciation
Composing Music	Designing a Building	Poetry
Creative Doodling	Drama	Understanding Conceptual Art
Creating Mind Map Art	Landscaping a Garden	Understanding the Human Language
Creative Thinking	Manifesting Thoughts	Writing a Book

Wellbeing:

Finding Happiness	Mental Health	Settling on a Treatment
Holistic Health	Physical Health	Spirituality
Life Planning	Self-analysis	Understanding Fears

Memory:

Brain Gymnastics	Improving Radiant Thinking	Recalling Learning
Capturing Knowledge	Mapping the Internal Cities of Thought	Recalling a Storyline or Plot
Improving Memory	Note-taking	Understanding a Text

A Mind Map Warm-up

This exercise is designed to ingrain the fundamental elements of Mind Mapping in your brain-cell patterns so that Mind Map mastery starts to become like second nature to you.

Taken in four stages, the initial "blitz" Mind Map releases the brain from the prison of self-editing, allowing for a rapidly upward learning curve to follow. Then, as you progress from spending 5 to 10 to 20 minutes on your Mind Maps, it will become apparent that once your brain really knows what a Mind Map is, it will be released to express its natural thoughts. Like a runner settling into their stride, the brain can then "breathe" much more freely and, in the longer exercises, inhale and exhale with increased pleasure and productivity.

Let's get started:

Read through the Top 99 Mind Map applications (see page 160).

Now pick a topic and make a Mind Map for it. Give yourself only 5 minutes in which to sketch out this Mind Map. The idea is to free yourself up in much the same way that artists often do a number of lightning-quick warm-up sketches before settling down to complete a masterpiece.

After a short break, pick another topic from a different category (e.g. "Education" rather than "Home"). Next, make a Mind Map in 10 minutes.

Repeat the process with a third topic from another category. Complete your Mind Map in 15 minutes.

Choose a fourth topic from one of the remaining categories. Finish this Mind Map in 20 minutes.

Compare the amount of detail and originality of the four Mind Maps as they progress from an earlier stage to a more developed stage. Then imagine how much more you would be able to generate if you had an hour to complete a solution-finding Mind Map.

Take another close look at the Mind Maps. Which one appeals to you the most? Why?

Now, or when you next have the opportunity, work on the Mind Map that appeals to you most until it looks completely finished to you, or use it as the basis for another Mind Map on the same topic.

ADVANCED MIND MAPPING AT HOME

This rest of this chapter explores some examples of how you can take your Mind Mapping practice a step further, using Mind Maps to handle complex and challenging situations as well as consider the bigger picture of what you want from all areas of your life.

Mind Mapping Planners

You can do more with Mind Maps than scope out the coming week. They also make great day-by-day planners; equally, they can be used to outline your schedule for a whole month or even a year. A Mind Map planner can be used both to plan your life and to review it; it can help you highlight your priorities and make sure you are in charge of your own time, achieving a healthy balance between work and leisure activities. Rather than becoming a slave to a schedule that's not of your own making or in your best interests, a Mind Map planner is a powerful way to make sure your days are literally full of colour!

My personal Mind Map day planner is full of images, codes, colours, keywords and key symbols. The most important topic of the day always inspires the central image. I usually use five main branches: "morning", "lunch", "afternoon", "evening" and "miscellaneous", although sometimes these main branches or events relating to them can generate five separate mini Mind Maps, circling the central Mind Map like satellites round a planet.

The central Mind Map connects with a sketch of a clock in the top left of the page (as described in the exercise on page 166). Images, symbols and codes are placed in the time slots of the clock, giving me an instant overview of what I would like to accomplish in the hours ahead. Unlike a conventional, linear planner, which might only lists the hours in a day from 8 a.m. until 6 p.m., the clocks in my Mind Map diary are divided into 24 hours. I choose to start my days at midnight because, like many other creative thinkers, I have found the brain can be very productive in the small hours. I could, for instance, decide to spend the hours between midnight and 3 a.m. concentrating on a new project, writing, Mind Mapping or solving problems.

The imagery in my Mind Map diary links in turn to my monthly schedule, so the two of them – diary and schedule – work in tandem like the cogs in a machine. My monthly schedule shows key images and words relating to the most important events in the month, as well as the on-going activities I enjoy, such as a running, rowing and lecturing

My diary entries and monthly schedules work symbiotically: the overview of the month triggers my memory of the days, and the days trigger memories of the month. Whenever I flick through my diary, it's like watching stills from the movie of my life.

Before I invented Mind Mapping and developed this way of keeping a combined diary and monthly schedule, I used to forget whole chunks of my life. Now, though, Mind Mapping keeps my memory fresh and I intend to carry on using it until the day I drop! And I hope, once you have taken the many benefits and pleasures of Mind Maps to heart, the same will go for you too!

Besides mapping out your monthly schedule, you can use a Mind Map to create a yearly planner. A yearly planner Mind Map could have a branch for each month of the year, while the sub-branches will relate to that month's most pressing concerns and considerations. It's a great way to plan for important events such as weddings, travel, trips and parties. I also use yearly planners to make sure my year ahead contains a healthy balance of work, travel, writing and leisure.

Hour by Hour

Try making a Mind Map planner entry for today.

Begin by drawing a clock in the top left-hand corner of your page. Divide this into 24 segments.

Fill the segments of the clock with appropriate words, images and codes, blocking out your use of time.

What is the most important thing you need to consider or achieve today? Use this to inspire the central image of your Mind Map. In the space below the clock, draw your central image, leaving plenty of room around it.

Now create branches from the central image, relating to the main areas or themes of your day. Colour these main branches in different colours. Create sub-branches from the main branches.

Link the main branches and sub-branches to the clock with connecting arrows where relevant, so that the two are working in harmony – like clockwork!

Are there any events, experiences or considerations that deserve to be made into mini Mind Maps of their own, circling the central Mind Map?

When you have finished, consider what perspectives the Mind Map offers on the way you use your time?

ADVANCED MIND MAPPING AT WORK

The business community has adopted Mind Mapping with incredible enthusiasm over the years. Sometimes this has produced mixed results: as we saw in Chapter 3, many of the diagrams that purport to be Mind Maps are not true Mind Maps at all. However, when the Laws are followed properly, Mind Maps can achieve spectacular results in the workplace, where they have an infinite range of applications, including researching projects, creating presentations, writing annual reports, managing time, brainstorming, negotiating and thinking strategically.

Scaling their applications up a notch, Mind Maps can be used to plan the vision for a company on a grand scale, and have other sophisticated uses, such as resolving company disputes (see page 169). On an individual basis they can help you decide which career path to pursue as well as plan how to climb the promotion ladder.

Decision Making

We saw in Chapter 4 how to tackle indecision when considering the outcome of a Mind Map. Here we are going to look at how Mind Maps can be very helpful in decision making itself, enabling you to see the pros and cons of any given situation at a glance. Of course this is a skill that is useful in any arena of life, but it is perhaps most valuable of all in the workplace.

Decisions that lead to simple yes/no responses are typically known as dyadic decisions (from the Latin *dyas*, meaning "two"). To use a Mind Map to help you make a dyadic decision, create it as you would any other Mind Map, starting with a strong central image and using your imagination, association and intuition to create main branches from it that relate to the most important considerations you wish to address.

When you are making a Mind Map to help you make a decision, be aware that the colours and pictures you allocate to the different branches will give you an insight into the subtle workings of your subconscious, perhaps revealing hidden preferences through the use of favourite colours for likes, or less favoured colours and images for dislikes.

When you have completed the Mind Map about your dilemma, take a moment to consider and try the following:

- **What feelings did creating the Mind Map give you? Did you have any particularly strong emotions when working on any of the branches? Or did any of them leave you feeling completely indifferent?**
- **Did you have an "aha" moment at any stage during the process? Could you sense a way forward before even completing the Mind Map?**
- **Rank each of the keywords on either side of the Mind Map with a number between 1 and 100 according to how important that word is. Tally up the score for the "yes" side and for the "no" side. Which total is highest? The highest total wins – but how do you feel about that outcome?**
- **If you are still unclear about the way forward, or your reaction to the plan of action suggested by the Mind Map, take some time out. Go away and incubate your response.**
- **If the above does not lead to a decision, recall the process described in Chapter 4 (see page 144), related to indecision.**

Whether you are deciding if you should redecorate your bedroom or move house, pursue a course of treatment proposed by your healthcare provider, or accept a new job, Mind Maps can act as a loyal companion along the way, helping you face life's big (and small) decisions with equanimity.

Mind Maps and the Art of Conflict Resolution

Mind Maps are usually created by individuals as highly personalized thinking tools, yet they can also be a very productive joint enterprise. At this more advanced level, they can be an extremely useful and rewarding way to explore another person's point of view in conjunction with your own, and for finding common ground and resolving disputes.

Before attempting to create a joint Mind Map to resolve a disagreement or upset, you need to gain enough experience in Mind Mapping to make the Laws feel as if they are part of the very fibre of your being!

That way, you will be absolutely certain of the process before attempting to guide anybody else through it.

There are two possible approaches to using Mind Mapping in conflict resolution. The first involves two or more people working together on a single Mind Map, taking turns to add branches, to explore associations and to discuss the approach. In the second method, the parties concerned work on separate Mind Maps, which are then shared, compared and discussed.

I have found that the best way to proceed is to present the problems first and then to follow these by the positives, before settling on solutions. This way, the discussion is more likely to remain upbeat and reach a positive conclusion instead of deteriorating in a spiral of negativity.

Whichever approach you take, it's important to allow everyone to have their say; to speak honestly and openly; and to respect everybody's opinions whether you agree with them or not. If the exchange becomes heated, take time out to cool down. Then resume the discussion by keeping the focus purely on the information in the Mind Map(s), rather than being tempted to resort to personal attacks or criticism.

As shown in the example *opposite*, a Mind Map for resolving conflict could start by defining the issue at hand, perhaps with each participant contributing keywords that summarize the situation for them. The next branch could explore the effects of the situation, covering positives (if any) as well as negatives, looking at areas such as the impact on the team and on personal feelings. You could then go on to address what you believe is needed to resolve the situation, as well as what you want (needs and wants are not necessarily the same thing). Finally, the Mind Map could explore solutions that build on the insights uncovered during the process.

Once the exchange is complete, a positive step forward could be to create a joint Mind Map based on the solutions you have reached. A possible approach is illustrated *opposite*, with the two participants each using an identifying colour (blue and red) to highlight their feelings and ideas, rather than each branch being given its own colour, as is more usual in Mind Mapping. Where feelings are mutual, both colours are used, and a third colour (purple) is used for the branch identifying the jointly reached solution.

WORK TO LIVE, LIVE TO WORK

I think I must be a strong contender for the person with the best job in the world: I get to meet fascinating people, travel the globe and share my passion for Mind Maps, witnessing first-hand how they radically transform the lives of others. It's pretty amazing, really! As adults, many of us spend most of our waking hours at work. In light of this, I believe it's important to find work that gives us a sense of achievement in some way, or feeds our sense of purpose. Here again, Mind Maps can help, as the following story by Maneesh Dutt shows.

MIND MAP FOR RESOLVING CONFLICT

The Courage to Start Out on My Own

Maneesh Dutt is a successful author, speaker and trainer.
He was working as a chemical engineer in Delhi when he realized
he needed to make some changes if he wanted to pursue a career
he truly loved. This is his story:

There is a "quiet" majority of company employees who
harbour an entrepreneurial ambition but who fail to garner
sufficient energy to push themselves in the direction
of their passions. I was no different, once upon a time.
Having being bitten by the Mind Mapping bug, I was
contemplating quitting my job to pursue this passion
24/7. However, with two decades of only regular job
experience behind me and no entrepreneurial experience,
this was by no means an easy decision to make and I had
my set of doubts and fears.

But it all changed on a quiet weekend when I decided to
Mind Map my challenge. I made a simple Mind Map with
four branches, as shown in the picture *opposite*.

In the first two branches (on the right), I analysed the pain
I was trying to avoid by not changing, and the pleasure I
was getting by continuing in the job. In the third branch,
I identified the pain that I would experience if I continued
in my current job for long. Finally, the last branch captured
the pleasure that I would achieve if I became a freelance
trainer/consultant for Mind Maps.

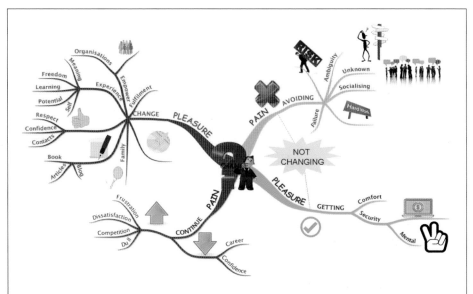

Mind Map by Maneesh Dutt on his career challenge

This Mind Map – and especially the final branch, which captured all my joyous emotions – gave me the much-needed courage to take the plunge and start out on my own without any further delay. So the following Monday I submitted my resignation and began my journey as a freelance trainer. I am happy to confirm that there has been no turning back: I am really experiencing all I had mapped, were I to make the change. I would strongly encourage others in a similar dilemma to give this sort of Mind Map a try.

Maneesh Dutt is now a highly successful global Mind Map instructor and the author of books including *Mind Maps for Effective Project Management*, which can be found on the shelves of the prestigious Harvard Business School library.

Devising a Company Vision

In 2015, Arab scientist and mathematician Dr Manahel Thabet achieved a Guinness World Record when she taught 1,350 students how to Mind Map in just 30 minutes. She is also the creator of a Super Mind Map that blew me away when I visited Dubai to see it. Manahel told me that after being awarded the World Record, she was approached by Abdulhamid Juma, Chairman of the Dubai International Film Festival (DIFF). He challenged her to create a Mind Map about the Dubai Film Festival's operations, reach and global positioning. In addition to this, Abdulhamid asked Manahel to invite me to sign the Mind Map when it was completed.

For three days, Manahel trained a team of managers from DIFF in Mind Mapping and worked with them on collecting and collating their data. No organization had ever attempted a project like this

Dr Thabet considering a draft of the DIFF Mind Map

It was a pleasure and a privilege to add my signature to the DIFF Mind Map.

before, and at first some team members were understandably sceptical about the process – to them it just looked like a confused mass of colours and squiggles. Initially they didn't believe that Mind Mapping could help improve their creativity, memory and intelligence.

Yet, by the end of the three days, they completely agreed. Manahel and her team then spent a whole day hand drawing the Mind Map. The result of their collaboration was a remarkable achievement. The DIFF Mind Map was complex, comprehensive, practical and followed the Laws of Mind Mapping to the last detail. It provided a comprehensive overview of the company at that point in time, while also highlighting areas for potential development and expansion, making it the perfect tool for guiding the company successfully into the future.

Manahel recalls how, while working on it, her shoulders ached so much that she felt like Michelangelo painting the dome of the Sistine Chapel! I told her that it was an honour to sign the DIFF Mind Map. The more I looked at it, the more magnificent it became. To the best of my knowledge, this was the first Mind Map to look at a subject in microcosmic and macrocosmic detail, mapping its past as well highlighting its possible futures.

ADVANCED MIND MAPPING FOR EDUCATION

In Chapter 2 I explained how Mind Maps are like soldiers in the battle against ignorance, empowering your brain with their artillery. Whether you are planning a speech, preparing a presentation or writing an essay, Mind Mapping is an excellent way to order and articulate your thoughts. They can be used for learning languages, advanced note-taking and précising complete works, as well as for essay writing and researching projects. If you have an educational goal, Mind Maps can help you achieve it.

Raymond Keene, OBE, is a British chess grandmaster, the chess correspondent for *The Times* and *Spectator*, and the most prolific author on chess and thinking in the history of the game. He created the Mind Map on page 178, which explains the history of the modern game of chess.

Learn Like a Native

Through the use of colour and imagery, Mind Mapping lifts language off the page and releases the brain, like a bird from a cage, to fly free in the realm of ideas and association. This is one reason why a Mind Map is an excellent means to learn a second language. When you were at school, did you have to memorize tedious, monochromatic lists of vocabulary? No wonder many of us found languages tricky to learn. Unlike linear teaching methods and mind-numbing columns of words, a Mind Map is an excellent way to learn new vocabulary.

The Mind Map has an advantage over other teaching methods in that it is a product of the Human Language itself (see Chapter 1, page 34): a Mind Map therefore instinctively transcends divisions in order to create links and connections between separate categories. Chunking can also be used very effectively in Mind Maps for language learning to group related information into memorable clusters, mirroring the way the brain processes information.

Vocab Test

Below is a selection of Swedish words and their English equivalents, presented in the list form so beloved of teachers everywhere.

Your mission – should you wish to accept it – is to create a Mind Map based on this vocabulary. Be sure to include colour, plenty of symbols and chunking where appropriate.

människa	human being	*valp*	puppy
man	man	*katt*	cat
kvinna	woman	*kattunge*	kitten
barn	child	*fågel*	bird
hund	dog	*fisk*	fish

Once you have created your Mind Map, spend about 20 minutes considering it and memorizing it.

When you are ready, cover up your Mind Map and the vocab list (no cheating!). Next, answer the following five questions:

What is the Swedish word for "human being"?

> **Kattunge is to katt as [_____] is to hund.**

What is the English word for kvinna?

> **Where would you expect to find a fågel – in the sky or in the sea?**

What is the Swedish word for "child"?

A Thinking Tool for Achievement

Take a close look at the Mind Map below. What does it tell you?

In it, chess grandmaster Raymond Keene charts the history of the chess game. He begins with games in the lost city of Ur, considers the Arabic cultivation of the game *shatranj* (a precursor of chess), charts the Renaissance changes to chess and concludes with Spanish influences, which resulted in the modern game.

The article on which the Mind Map is based is over 1,000 words long, and tracks 5,000 years of history, yet Raymond's Mind Map makes all that information available at a glance. In his own words:

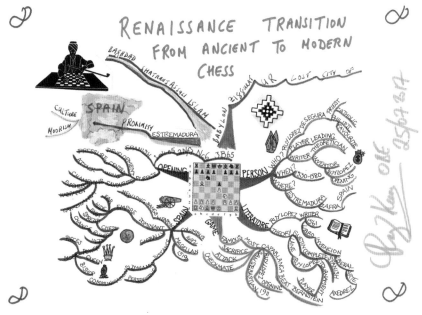

Mind Map on the transition to modern chess by Raymond Keene

The virtue of a Mind Map when preparing a speech or writing an article is twofold: the writer is constantly stimulated by the branching trees of ideas to new and more daring thoughts; while at the same time the keywords and central images ensure that in the verbiage of speaking and writing, no major point is overlooked.

The Mind Map is particularly useful in this context. Without turning or shuffling any pages, it is possible to inform the audience in advance about the structure and key points. Because you are always operating from one sheet, you can tell your audience what you plan to say, you can say it with confidence, and then you can recap to demonstrate you have proved your point. With linear notes, the danger is ending simply where the notes stop, in essence a random moment, often determined by chronology rather than meaning.

Assuming that the lecturer has complete command of their subject, the keywords act as a catalyst for enthusiasm and extempore ideas instead of a dry recitation of facts often determined by dates rather than significant content (i.e. the lecture starts at the beginning of the subject's life and finishes at the end). If the lecturer does not have perfect grasp of the subject, linear notes simply make it worse. Whether writing an article or giving a verbal lecture, the Mind Map acts like a ship's helm to navigate through the main oceans of the presentation.

ADVANCED MIND MAPPING FOR CREATIVITY

If you have been creating Mind Maps for the exercises in this book, I hope it will be clear to you by now that you are naturally creative: you have been engaging your faculties of association and imagination to create highly individual and unique Mind Maps that express the workings of your brain.

I have seen many Mind Maps that are wonderful works of art in their own right, with dazzling colours and inventive imagery. Regardless of whether a Mind Maps falls into this category, it can inspire masterpieces. It can, for example, be used to shape a sculpture or map out the movements in a piece of music, as well provide inspiration for works of poetry and prose.

WRITE LIKE A POET

You may think that poetry is something only "poets" can attempt, but with the help of a Mind Map you too can find your muse. Poetry has been one of the driving forces of my own life. In Chapter 2, I encouraged you to learn a limerick by Edward Lear. *Opposite* is an exercise that invites you to write a piece of your own. First, though, I would like to share a simple piece of mine in which the imagery flows like a branch in a Mind Map:

> **Happy sparrow**
> **Doing somersaults;**
> **Autumn leaf**
> **Tumbling in**
> **Springtime**
> **Winds.**

As you can see, it is a very short poem that is rather like a Japanese haiku in its simplicity and focus, although it is free from a haiku's formal three-line structure. I've shared it to make the point that you don't have to choose a

Meet Your Muse

Here is an exercise to get you started on a poem of your own. Start by choosing one of the following randomly selected words:

rose	winter	water
bridge	cloud	fall
sleep	puzzle	touch
leaf	glass	knife
sand	rope	touch
mouse	sandwich	love
fur	dream	

Once you have chosen your word, make a Mind Map about it. Push the branches, sub-branches and sub-sub-branches in this Mind Map as far as you can, right to the edges of the paper, using colours, images, codes and connecting arrows.

Which branches stand out the most?

Which images catch your eye and ignite your imagination?

What connections intrigue you the most?

Use these stimuli as the basis of a short poem.

grand subject or an elaborate rhyme scheme to write a poem that means something to you. Follow the instructions on page 181 to Mind Map a simple topic and prepare to meet your inner poet!

Get Published!

As you may have noticed, many of my fellow Mind Mappers have gone on to become published authors. If you are thinking about writing a book of your own, use a Mind Map to plan your approach. These days, if you want your book to be a success, you need to think about more than the subject matter. Use your branches and sub-branches to consider topics such as:

- **The concept of the book: the initial spark of your idea, your approach and your ambitions for it. Do you want it to inform, surprise and/or entertain?**
- **Research you need to do before you start writing: this could be into your chosen genre, the market (what's the competition?), your readership (age and gender, for example) as well as background information needed for the text itself.**
- **Your plan for the elements of your book, such as (if you are writing fiction) plot, characters and themes, as well as your writing schedule and target word count.**
- **The writing process itself, including a schedule for the drafts as well as where you will find encouragement and feedback.**
- **How you will promote the book and yourself as an author. This includes ways of connecting with your audience and building a platform to promote your work through, for example, social media, and a personal blog and website.**
- **Finally, you might want to look at whether you want to go the traditional publishing route or try self-publishing, weighing factors such as cost, profit, speed, support and artistic freedom against one another.**

MIND MAP FOR GETTING PUBLISHED

Apply Design Thinking Principles

Design thinking is a methodology that has come to the fore in recent years as a practical, creative and solution-based way of reasoning. The stages usually include a variation on:

Empathise – learn from people
Define – find patterns
Ideate – design principles
Prototype – make tangible
Test – iterate

It can be applied to systems, procedures, protocols and customer experiences. Rather than concentrating on fixing problems, it is an action-oriented process that focuses on finding desirable outcomes, and which takes into consideration empathy and emotions. It also calls upon logic, imagination and intuition. (Remind you of anything yet?)

The design mindset is about building up ideas until an "aha" moment is reached, when the path forward becomes clear. As design thinking involves making things visible and tangible, drawing is one of its main tools for working through ideas, sharing, dialogue and communication. *Opposite* is a Mind Map exploring the application of basic design thinking principles.

It can come as no surprise, then, that Mind Maps play an integral role in the design thinking method. After all, a Mind Map is all about imagination and building up ideas through making them visible on the page. Moreover, a Mind Map is *itself* a design: it is thinking made visible! Mind Maps and mini Mind Maps can be applied at every stage of the design process – from the inception of a design to its practical realization – and can be used to design anything from the planting scheme of a garden to a plan for expanding a business to the outline of your ideal life.

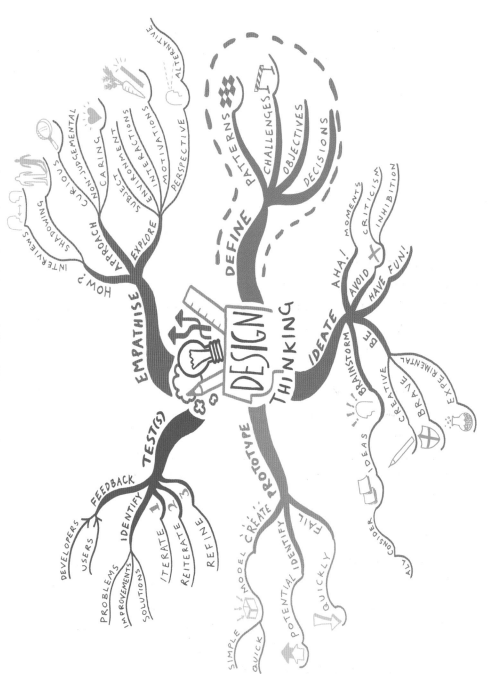

ADVANCED MIND MAPPING FOR WELLBEING

We have seen how Mind Maps can act like your very own personal trainer (see Chapter 2, page 114) by helping you to plan a fitness regime or enjoy a healthy diet.

Besides their use in promoting general wellbeing, Mind Maps have been shown to be effective in engaging with a number of conditions, such as autism and dyslexia. People on the autistic spectrum often have strong visual skills, which means that autistic children tend to learn better through visual methods. Mind Maps are, of course, highly visual and encourage a learning-by-doing approach. They offer an overview of a subject, as well as emphasizing the relationships between different aspects of it, making information appear orderly and helping autistic students to improve their recall of that information. For those with dyslexia, short-term memory, concentration and sequencing information can all be challenging aspects of daily life, so Mind Maps offer them a helpful way to organize and assimilate information.

For those suffering from depression and states of demotivation, a Mind Map can highlight symptoms, outline coping techniques and strategies, and include helpful medical information on the biological causes. It becomes an action plan as well as a diagnostic tool. Wherever stress can lead to forgetfulness, rigidity and a downward spiral of fear, Mind Maps can act as stress relievers, massaging that stress away. When the brain is less stressed, the body becomes less stressed, leading to improved performance and mental and physical wellbeing.

Mind Maps can be used generally to improve your understanding of a condition and then devise a helpful treatment plan. If, for example, you are creating a Mind Map to manage anxiety, you could start with a central

Kate Swaffer's Story

When Kate Swaffer was diagnosed with dementia at the age of 49, she was advised by professionals to leave her job, get her affairs in order and to make the most of whatever time she had left. Just under a decade later, she had completed two undergraduate degrees, an MSc and was studying for a PhD.

Today, Kate is a published poet, author and internationally acclaimed spokesperson for the millions of people around the world who live with dementia. In 2017, she was awarded the accolade of Australian of the Year for South Australia and her phenomenal campaigning work continues to take her all over the world.

Kate is an advocate of non-pharmacological interventions and Mind Maps form an important part of her armoury. She was introduced to Mind Mapping in 2007 by her disability advisor at the University of South Australia and has described on her blog how she could not function as well as she does without Mind Maps: "… as they map things out visually, offering another way to find my way". Her story is a humbling example of the way in which Mind Maps can help a courageous individual like Kate live a fulfilling life in the face of a diagnosis such as dementia.

image that relates to your feelings, then create main branches and sub-branches relating to:

- **things that trigger your anxiety**
- **how anxiety affects your life**
- **things that are counterproductive or exacerbate your anxiety**
- **activities that help you manage it**
- **support from family, friends and professionals**

Mind Maps can be useful for carers too. They can, for example, be used to record notes about important aspects of a person's life, such as their preferred lifestyle and the significant individuals or events in their lives. Besides their social function, Mind Maps can be used medically as a means of arranging and agreeing the details of care and treatment plans.

THE FIGHT AGAINST DEMENTIA

As storehouses or even giant warehouses of information, Mind Maps can help hold the fort in the battle against such devastating conditions as dementia. They can be used by those who have been given a diagnosis of dementia as well as those who care for them.

In 2010, American research psychologist Dr George Huba was diagnosed with an untreatable, early-onset neurodegenerative disease and dementia. He was told that he had little time left. A year later, he retired from his job as an evaluator of health and social care programmes. However, he had no intention of resigning himself to his condition. Instead, he drew on his professional experience to research visual thinking methods for those with cognitive decline who wish to minimize its impact on their future.

Dr Huba soon found that Mind Mapping provided an especially effective and inexpensive way of ordering his daily life and memories, making decisions and planning for the future. By getting rid of complex sentence structures and the need to learn by rote, Mind Maps appeal to the mind in the present moment. Today, George Huba writes an engaging blog about "My Life as an Ongoing Cognitive and Medical Experiment", enjoys a large following on Twitter and has published a short book called *Mind Mapping, Cognitive Impairment, and Dementia* (*Huba's Bolero*). He is a pioneer in the use of Mind Maps as a tool to tackle the effects of cognitive decline.

For those who have dementia, Mind Maps offer a visual thinking tool with which to record memories, organize daily routines and plan ahead. They can be used, for instance, for choosing meals and clothing, for remembering medications, and as Mind Map diaries and schedule planners. They can help Mind Mappers with dementia remember medical appointments and visitors. Some people with dementia may be able to express themselves more easily through pictures, sketches and scribbles than in words, in which instance the Mind Map can act as a useful communication device to help them relate to the people they love and the people who care for them.

Mind Maps help dementia sufferers and those who support them make the most of the present moment.

ADVANCED MIND MAPPING FOR MEMORY

In 1991, Ray Keene and I co-founded the World Memory Championships, an event that is separate from the World Mind Mapping Championships but also falls in the field of Mind Sports, and forms part of my life's work in promoting and improving global mental literacy. Today, competitors from all over the world take part in the Championships; it's a truly multicultural event. The Championships consist of ten different disciplines in which the participants memorize as much information as possible within a given period of time, such as the order of a pack of cards or a long sequence of binary numbers.

World champion mnemonist Dominic O'Brien featured in the *Guinness Book of Records* for his achievement on 1 May 2002, when he committed to memory a random sequence of 2,808 playing cards after looking at each card only once. As he explained earlier in this chapter (see page 157), Mind Maps are an essential part of his toolkit.

We have seen how Mind Maps can be used to memorize information. They can also be used as productive exercises in their own right with which to improve your memory by giving your brain a healthy workout.

A Mind Map of Mind Mapping

This wonderful Mind Map relates to the processes of Mind Mapping itself. It was created by Chinese Mind Mapper Liu Yan, and helped her win a well-deserved gold medal in the 2016 World Mind Mapping Championships. Liu Yan has placed a portrait of me as the central image, and has created branches relating to key aspects of Mind Mapping such as its methodology, its applications, and the means by which it is created through drawing, the use of 3D and the Laws of Mind Mapping (see Chapter 2, page 60). The resulting Mind Map is imaginative, witty, colourful and a delight to behold. It is full of humorous touches that make memorizing it easy and fun.

Talk the Talk

This next exercise will enable you to experience the ways in which Mind Mapping can help you to read faster, improve your understanding, take useful notes and offer an overview of the material you are reading – as well as memorize that information.

- **Pick a book from your shelves and open it at random.**
- **Flick through it until you get to the next new chapter or main section of text. Skim through this to get an overview of its contents.**
- **Now sketch out a draft Mind Map.**
- **If you need to, refer to the seven steps of Mind Mapping in Chapter 1, page 28, and the Laws of Mind Mapping in Chapter 2, page 60.**
- **Review the text for more gold and refine your Mind Map. Keep looking at the text as you do this to be sure you've included everything you need.**
- **Close the book.**
- **Using only your Mind Map, recall the subject of the text in as much detail as you can.**

Most people feel note-taking slows you down when you read. The Mind Map does exactly the opposite for you: when your Mind Map is fine-tuned to the keywords in a text, your eye–brain system will search out, like a detective, the key elements of the content – immediately forming a network of associations that will give you the 'aha!' experience of understanding. As you refine your Mind Map, you will refine your understanding.

Creating Magic

When Liu Yan won the 2016 World Mind Mapping Championships, I was in awe of her work. She had managed to create what could only be described as a Mind Mapping masterpiece in a highly pressurized environment, with very limited time. I remember telling the audience: "Whether you're from China or another country, please learn Mind Mapping from Miss Liu, because she is surely one of the leading figures in the Mind Map field!" Here's Liu's story in her own words …

My name is Liu Yan, and I come from Beijing. I have been teaching Mind Mapping in China since 2009. I became interested in Mind Maps the first time I came across them in a book by Tony Buzan. At the age of 23, I took the lead in drawing a giant Mind Map ($600m^2$), which was spread out on Baiyun Mountain in Guangzhou during the 19th World Memory Championship in 2009.

I met Mr Buzan for the first time in 2011, when he was giving a speech. As I was in the audience, I was not allowed to come into contact with him. However, when his speech ended, I managed to reach the stage with my Mind Map in my hands, despite the staff attempting to prevent me. And Mr Buzan exhibited his generosity in patiently giving me instructions. It was from that moment on that I decided to devote my professional career – in fact my whole life – to spreading and passing on this magical tool.

Mind Map on the processes of Mind Mapping by Liu Yan

So I came all the way to England to study Mind Mapping with Mr Buzan in August 2014, and I became the first qualified female Mind Map supervisor on the Chinese mainland. To date, I have taught over 60,000 students! The youngest student I have ever taught was only six years old. After my instruction, she was able to Mind Map a wonderful speech and then deliver it on stage. By studying Mind Maps, many of my students are able to improve their performance and become more efficient in their work.

In 2015, I organized 81 students in planning and drawing another giant Mind Map which, at 120m², was the biggest Mind Map in China at the time. I could not wait to send the picture of the map to Mr Buzan the minute it was done. On seeing the map, Mr Buzan gave it the highest praise, saying, "Unprecedented!"

A year later, in August 2016, I beat this record by leading 189 students in completing another giant Mind Map, 216m², in two hours and 20 minutes. The theme of this Mind Map was Chinese Excellent Traditional Culture, and it was reported by the *People's Daily* website.

I have gone on to create other giant Mind Maps with my students, including in 2017 a Mind Map of China itself, with the 34 provinces defined as units. Its creation symbolizes an attempt to unite Western and Eastern cultures. In China today, Mind Mapping has become a learning tool that many primary and middle -chool students have to master, and it is also a necessary skill for the employees of many large enterprises. I want to play my own part in handing down Mind Mapping to the coming generations in China, and I have now written two books on the subject of Mind Mapping, one of which is an introduction to Mind Mapping and another which relates Mind Maps to the ancient principles of the Tao-te-Ching.

On 12 December, 2016, I participated in the World Mind Mapping Championships in Singapore. After fierce competition, playing three games a day, I broke the record with the score of 92.5 in an event for speed-reading magazine articles and presenting their information in the form of Mind Maps. I also set new records for the other two events, spending an average of half an hour on each one. The moment when Mr Tony Buzan said, "The winner of this year's World Mind Mapping Championships gold medal is Liu Yan," I burst into tears. This prize is the best recognition that I could ever have hoped to achieve, both for myself and for my dear students.

Looking forward, I dream of helping more and more people benefit from this magical tool. I intend to devote myself to the Mind Map and the future looks bright!

I hope by now you will be excited and intrigued by the possibilities that Mind Maps can offer you in every aspect of life. From humble beginnings sketched on an A4 sheet of paper right up to Mind Maps so huge they cover mountainsides, there is literally no limit to where Mind Maps can take you, or the applications for them.

6

The Future
of Mind Mapping

What does the future hold for the
Mind Map? This chapter considers
the Mind Map in a digital age and its
potential relationship with developing
Artificial Intelligence. It looks at the
future of Mind Mapping and how it can
help smooth the path of your own life.

What's Next?

The Mind Map is evolving. This should come as no surprise, as a Mind Map mirrors the thinking processes of the human brain and the human brain is, of course, inevitably subject to the principles of evolution.

We saw in Chapter 1 how the Mind Map fits into the trajectory of history, taking its place in a chain of events triggered by the groundbreaking marks made by Stone Age artists millennia ago. We can now externalize by hand the Mind Maps that exist biologically within us, in the very fabric of our being, in the connections of our brain cells. Through drawing, writing and making marks, the Mind Map has emerged from the brain and on to the page.

Yet, in our new era, the balance appears to all intents and purposes to be shifting from the handmade to the computer generated, and researchers are now studying the ways in which our minds and thinking processes could be affected by developments in modern technology.

I am intrigued to see where the future will take us – and to discover what roles Mind Mapping will play in a world where Human Intelligence (HI) gets to grips with the implications of Artificial Intelligence (AI).

Going Digital

It's hard to believe that it's now over a decade since I teamed up with Chris Griffiths to create the first effective digital Mind Mapping software: iMindMap. A leading entrepreneur who sold his first company at the tender age of 26, Chris is the founder of OpenGenius, the company behind the iMindMap, which is now used by over one million people around the world. Together, we came up with software that reflects the brain's organic nature and the ways in which our thought processes interact – while obeying the Laws of Mind Mapping.

Unfortunately, many of the other apps and software packages that claim to be Mind Mapping tools break most of the Laws. In these instances, the software often generates concept maps in which, for example, the use of colour is optional and there are many "central" ideas; or a number of words or phrases are erroneously crammed into boxes and placed along the branches. In this sort of diagram, branches are not always connected, differentiated or ordered hierarchically.

It is always worth checking and comparing the matrix of the Mind Mapping Laws with the mini matrix of software programs that purport to be about Mind Mapping. If the two do not correlate, the program will not create a true Mind Map. As we have seen, the Laws of Mind Mapping are based on sound psychological principles, which means that the further a person deviates from them, the less effective the resulting diagram will be.

THE BENEFITS OF DIGITAL MIND MAPPING

By following the Laws of Mind Mapping, iMindMap software generates true Mind Maps – creating the necessary conditions for good thinking, creativity and excellent recall. The program has proved to be a particularly effective tool for use in brainstorming, negotiating, taking minutes, creating polished presentations and developing strategy.

The benefits of computer Mind Maps include:
- **They can be edited where necessary**
- **They can be backed up digitally**
- **Their clear graphics mean they are easy to read**
- **They can be linked to other multimedia**
- **They facilitate post-process analysis (for example, by going back over the stages)**
- **They are simple to generate using the supplied drawing tools and icons**

One of the undeniable bonuses of digital Mind Mapping is, of course, the speed and ease with which neat and useful documents can be shared electronically with colleagues – and even annotated by them where appropriate, encouraging collaboration within teams.

WHERE NEXT?

Like its human counterparts, iMindMap continues to evolve with the times and the emergence of new technologies. Yet for all of its advances in recent years, I believe that we are still only at the very beginning of Mind Mapping's digital adventure.

ROBOT LAWS VS THE LAWS OF MIND MAPPING

In 1950, American science fiction writer Isaac Asmiov published a prescient collection of short stories called *I, Robot*. In the 1942 story "Run Around" he introduced the "Three Laws of Robotics": 1. A robot may not injure a human being or, through inaction, allow a human being to come to harm; 2. A robot must obey the orders given it by human beings except where such orders would conflict with the First Law; 3. A robot must protect its own existence as long as such protection does not conflict with the First or Second Laws.

There are some people today who would argue that we have reached a point where we need to start actively putting some form of robotic laws in place – devising a sort of Ten Commandments for AI, if you will. On first consideration, their fears could seem justified: in June 2017, Ahmed Elgammal, Bingchen Liu, Mohamed Elhoseiny and Marian Mazzone – researchers at Rutgers University's Art and Artificial Intelligence (AI) Laboratory – published a paper in which they shared thought-provoking findings. The team had conducted an experiment in which a new computational system generated entirely new artworks. These pieces were then exhibited at Art Basel 2016 – and were preferred by many people who viewed them to the human-made art on display!

While that may be so, I believe that we have a long way to go before much of the hype surrounding AI is actualized, and I am more inclined to agree with the observations of Professor Gary Marcus, an American research psychologist whose work focuses on language, biology and the mind. In an article for the *New York Times* called "Artificial Intelligence Is Stuck. Here's How to Move It Forward" (29 July, 2017), he notes that AI systems struggle in the real world, and argues that we need to develop a new AI paradigm in which "top down" and "bottom up" knowledge are placed on an equal footing. He defines bottom-up knowledge as the sort of raw information we get directly from our senses, whereas top-down knowledge comprises cognitive models of how the world works. AI presently works primarily with top-down knowledge, rather than sensory stimulus. His argument is that both forms of knowledge need to be integrated if AI systems are to become anything more than passive receptacles for information. Computers today are not aware of what they are doing; they lack true consciousness, so are ultimately only as capable as their programmers are skilled. At the time of writing, they lack cognitive awareness.

I mentioned earlier that I am intrigued to see what the future holds for the Mind Map. While many believe that the world will inevitably be held hostage by the inexorable rise of AI (think of all those *Terminator* movies), I have yet to be convinced that robots can approach the beautiful organic complexity of the human brain. We have already developed skilful Mind Map software that can be used for stunning presentations, but we have yet to develop AI that can itself Mind Map by using association and imagination in meaningful ways – let alone do so while being conscious of the fact that this is what it is doing. Today, even supposedly "super robots" lack the ability to discriminate or are prone to falling flat on their faces when they can't see a step!

Rather than create new robotic laws, I would like to see the development of AI that is capable of consciously mastering the Laws of Mind Mapping, as I believe this is something that would represent a true challenge and, if achieved, an incredible accomplishment. As we have seen, through the use of imagination, logic, association and individual interpretation of the world, the Laws of Mind Mapping are inextricably intertwined with the fundamental principles of good thinking. While we have made significant advances with iMindMap and it will continue to go from strength to strength, I have yet to meet a robot that can create a Mind Map independently from human input.

I sincerely believe that the ability to make a Mind Map would act as the ultimate proof of intelligence in a robotic being.

A PROVOCATIVE CONVERSATION

My conversations with Polish Mind Mapping master Marek Kasperski always leave me feeling inspired and excited about the possibilities for this ultimate thinking tool. We recently found ourselves talking about digital Mind Mapping and AI, and Marek surprised me with a revelation.

"When I first looked at iMindMap, I liked it very much, but I found it wanting, to be honest," he confessed. "The principles are great but the Mind Map software on its own is two-dimensional – very flat. Not much in our world is very flat; it's all three-dimensional."

I could see his point.

Marek continued: "I started thinking about a central theme being like holding somebody's brain. It's a three-dimensional thing: I can spin it around and look at it from every different angle. Then I imagined the branches of the major themes coming out from it like tendrils. Not in a two-dimensional way, like they are on an iMindMap, but three-dimensional. So I would love to see a computer program that is 3D, where you can spin the Mind Map around. It would be like solar flares coming from the sun. They don't just move in one direction; they come towards you; they come away from you. If you could turn that around you could see this beautiful 3D Mind Map – like the three-dimensional, tiered game of chess that Spock plays in *Star Trek*."

He went on to share with me his thoughts on the benefits of developing completely 3D Mind Map software that can be used on a screen or a tablet, and spun with your finger, helping you to understand the spatial potential of a Mind Map, with all its different branches flowing out in a 360-degree sphere.

We are now in the process of refining 3D iMindMap software – and the opportunities are boundless.

AI itself is often approached as a game of numbers; big numbers admittedly. Even something as apparently straightforward as a game of chess can involve 10 to the power of 70 possible moves (which gives a figure of 10 with 70 noughts after it), which is why it took decades and billions of dollars for IBM to develop a supercomputer called Deep Blue that was capable of beating then world chess champion Garry Kasparov in 1997.

Another further challenge for AI came in the form of the abstract strategy board game Go. Many in the robotic community believed AI couldn't master Go, as this game has 10 to the power of 170 possible moves. The complexity is phenomenal. However, British AI researcher Demis Hassabis was determined to tackle the problem. Besides being a researcher, neuroscientist and computer game designer, he is a Mind Mapper and two-time winner of the Decamentathlon, a multidisciplinary Mind Sports event. He is also the co-founder of DeepMind, a company dedicated to pushing the frontiers of AI technologies. And, although it took time, with the backing of Internet giant Google, DeepMind succeeded in developing an AI program called AlphaGo that, in 2014, proved capable of beating a world-class Go champion.

As AI has beaten the top two athletes in the field of Mind Sports, there are those who believe it must be close to overtaking us. But let's think back to those numbers games for a moment. A Mind Map radiates branches (BOIs) from its centre. From each main branch, more branches grow, and from each of those branches yet more branches potentially appear … The question is how many theoretical, possible branches could spring from any one branch – and the answer, of course, stretches toward infinity. Even in two dimensions, the potential reach of a Mind Map is incalculable.

So, rather than concentrating on developing Mind Mapping software, we could flip the coin on its head. Instead of using digital technologies to push the parameters of Mind Mapping, Mind Mapping could prove a way to push the potential of AI itself.

During my conversation with Marek, I confessed my vision for the future of Mind Mapping, which entails establishing a new AI software multimillion dollar prize in much the same way that there have been prizes for the development of AI in the fields of Mind Sports such as chess.

Sponsored by AI pioneers in the way that Deep Blue was created by IBM and Deep Mind was supported by Google, this prize would be awarded to the first AI program or supercomputer that could follow the Laws of Mind Mapping in order to create its own self-generated Mind Map. In addition to this, the program would be able to replicate the way in which humans can master and apply Mind Mapping in practical ways. This ground-breaking program would:

- **Create hundreds of Mind Maps in different forms using different images**
- **Understand the Mind Maps that it generates**
- **Demonstrate that it can think**
- **Communicate the ideas captured in the Mind Map, expressing it in different languages, or using other words that direct the listening intelligence to the same goal in the way that a human Mind Mapper can communicate information captured in Mind Map form**
- **Express the ideas in the Mind Map by translating them into art, sculpture or music in the same way that real people can use Mind Maps to inspire their creative accomplishments**

Hearing this, Marek smiled and reminded me that at this stage in the history of AI, even an allegedly sophisticated robot is primarily a device that mimics other things in such a way that it convinces you it is thinking for itself, yet it is not. It is merely a unit processing binary numbers: ones and zeros, "yes" and "no", one or the other. But it is not thinking: it is reacting and calculating – but not thinking. Nor is it feeling for that matter.

I agreed with Marek's observations, and noted that, after losing to Deep Blue, Garry Kasparov observed that, rather than being disappointed by the outcome, he was more saddened by the fact that the poor machine had beaten the world's greatest chess player, yet hadn't the faintest idea of what it was doing and didn't even know it had won.

Nor could it do what he, then world chess champion, would be doing later: Deep Blue would never enjoy a nice meal, listen to the environment around it, laugh, cry and reminisce, while at the same time remembering all the moves in the game. Unlike him, it hadn't lived every millisecond of that game.

As the situation stands, it seems that a human element will remain an essential component in Mind Mapping for the foreseeable future. But if Mind Mapping could be used in the practical development of AI – as a means to stretch it, challenge it and grow it – imagine how wonderful that would be. And if Mind Mapping can do that for AI, just imagine in what amazing ways it could help you improve your own life. As a human being, you are a super biocomputer and your potential is incredible.

Your Future

When my book *Use Your Head* was first published by the BBC, I was called into the publishing offices. My editor greeted me with an embarrassed smile. "I have a confession to make: your book seems to disappear from the shelves here more than any other title. Not only is *Use Your Head* selling like hot cakes, but copies vanish into thin air as soon as they arrive from the warehouse!"

I laughed. I was delighted by the thought that my book was "disappearing" and that copies were being taken home by staff eager to learn how to use their heads and improve their brainpower.

Over the years, however, others have misappropriated Mind Mapping in ways that have not always been so benign. Witnessing the misuse and misinterpretation of the Mind Map has, at times, felt a bit like travelling on a coach that's been held up by a highwayman; then watching a precious treasure being carried away and buried in the woods where it can't benefit anybody.

My primary concern – and one of the motivations for writing this book – is to ensure that the integrity of this amazing thinking tool is neither lost nor compromised, and that it goes on to help millions more people around the world today and in the future. Having devoted my adult life to teaching and sharing the Mind Map, my wish is that *Mind Map Mastery* will show everybody what the Mind Map truly is, how it evolved and how it can help us individually; and that it will reinforce the fact that the Laws have a purpose and are there for a reason, because they are integral to good thinking.

Whatever your circumstances, the challenges you face, or your hopes and ambitions, you will find techniques and insights in this book that will enable you to become a true Mind Map master. It is my sincere belief that, once you have worked through the exercises in this book and gone on to master the art of Mind Mapping, you will be well on the way to mastering the art of life itself.

Embark on the next stage of your Mind Mapping adventure right now by making a "Change Your Life" Mind Map. In this Mind Map, draw upon all the Mind Mapping skills that you have acquired so far to look beyond your present circumstances, articulate your dreams and discover new, exciting ways in which to realize them. Once you begin, I know there will be no stopping you …

All that remains for me now is to wish you every success and happiness with the most potent thinking tool in the world to empower you.

Welcome to the Mind Mapping global family!

Resources

Tony Buzan – Inventor of Mind Mapping

www.tonybuzan.com

Welcome to Tony Buzan's world. Tony Buzan is the Inventor of Mind Maps – the most powerful "thinking tool" of our times. Discover more about Tony himself, and the transformative powers of Mind Mapping, memory and speed-reading, among other helpful resources.

iMindMap

www.imindmap.com

iMindMap is the first Mind Mapping, brainstorming and project planning software. It enables you to work creatively using five views including Fast Capture View, Brainstorm View, Mind Map View and Time Map View that help capture, organize, develop, action and launch your ideas. The software is used by many of the world's leading organizations, including Disney, the BBC, Nasa, Intel and Microsoft.

World Memory Championships

www.worldmemorychampionships.com

Founded by Tony Buzan and Raymond Keene OBE in 1991, when the first World Memory Championships was staged, this is a common competition framework that has enabled international competition to take place in the field of Memory Sports. It is based on the ten memory disciplines.

World Mind Mapping Council

www.worldmindmappingcouncil.com

Founded by Phil Chambers and Tony Buzan, the World Mind Mapping Council is dedicated to promoting the teaching of Mind Mapping worldwide and to advancing the course of global literacy.

REFERENCES

Collins, Allan M. and M. Ross Quillian "Retrieval Time From Semantic Memory", in *Journal of Verbal Learning and Verbal Behavior*, Elsevier, volume 8, 1969.

Elgammal, Ahmed, Bingchen Liu, Mohamed Elhoseiny, and Marian Mazzone, "CAN: Creative Adversarial Networks, Generating "Art" by Learning About Styles and Deviating from Style Norms", (available online) June 2017.

Farrand, Paul, Fearzana Hussain and Enid Hennessy, "The Efficacy of the "Mind Map" Study Technique", (available online) 2002.

Haber, Ralph, "How We Remember What We See", *Scientific American*, May 1970.

Huba, George, *Mind Mapping, Cognitive Impairment, and Dementia (Huba's Bolero)*, (available online) 2015.

Marcus, Gary, "Artificial Intelligence is Stuck. Here's How to Move It Forward", *New York Times*, July 29, 2017.

Restorff, Hedwig von, "The Effects of Field Formation in the Trace Field", 1933.

Toi, H., "Research on How Mind Map Improves Memory", paper presented at the International Conference on Thinking, Kuala Lumpur, 2009.

Index

Acknowledgements

The Publisher would like to thank Sue Lascelles for her invaluable assistance in creating this book.

The Publisher would like to thank the following Mind Mappers and photographic libraries for permission to reproduce their material. Every care has been taken to trace copyright holders. However, if we have omitted anyone, we apologize and will, if informed, make corrections to any future edition. All Mind Maps remain the copyright of their creators as listed below:

Page 26 Shutterstock; page 36 Shutterstock; page 37 Shutterstock; page 42 Shutterstock; page 43 (above) Shutterstock; page 43 (below) Shutterstock; page 44 Shutterstock; page 45 (below) Alamy; page 51 Shutterstock; page 126 Shutterstock; page 127 Shutterstock; page 128 (above) Shutterstock; page 128 (below) Shutterstock; page 129 Shutterstock; page 105 Mind Map by Marek Kasperski; page 113 Mind Map by Phil Chambers; page 132 Mind Map by Richard Lin; page 158 Mind Map by Dominic O'Brien; page 173 Mind Map by Maneesh Dutt; page 174 Manahel Thabet; page 175 Manahel Thabet; page 178 Mind Map by Raymond Keene; page 193 Mind Map by Liu Yan

WATKINS

Sharing Wisdom Since 1893

The story of Watkins began in 1893, when scholar of esotericism John Watkins founded our bookshop, inspired by the lament of his friend and teacher Madame Blavatsky that there was nowhere in London to buy books on mysticism, occultism or metaphysics. That moment marked the birth of Watkins, soon to become the publisher of many of the leading lights of spiritual literature, including Carl Jung, Rudolf Steiner, Alice Bailey and Chögyam Trungpa.

Today, the passion at Watkins Publishing for vigorous questioning is still resolute. Our stimulating and groundbreaking list ranges from ancient traditions and complementary medicine to the latest ideas about personal development, holistic wellbeing and consciousness exploration. We remain at the cutting edge, committed to publishing books that change lives.

DISCOVER MORE AT:

www.watkinspublishing.com

Read our blog

Watch and listen to
our authors in action

Sign up to
our mailing list

We celebrate conscious, passionate, wise and happy living.
Be part of that community by visiting

 /watkinspublishing   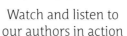 @watkinswisdom

/watkinsbooks   @watkinswisdom